MW00774215

ESSAYS *of a* BIOLOGIST

by
JULIAN HUXLEY

1887- 1975

New York
ALFRED · A · KNOPF
1923

Set up, electrotyped, printed and bound by the Vail-Ballou Press, Inc , Binghamton, N. Y.
Paper furnished by W. F. Etherington & Co , New York.

TO MY COLLEAGUES AND FRIENDS
AT THE RICE INSTITUTE
HOUSTON, TEXAS

PREFACE

A PREFACE should be long, like one of Mr. Shaw's, or short. I propose the latter.

The essays here collected were written on very various occasions. This must excuse the considerable overlap that will be found among them. I have not thought it worth while to attempt to get rid of this, since, though facts may be repeated, the point of view and general context are on each occasion different.

Contrary to all custom, I have put the meat courses ι at the two ends of my menu. If an author may presume to advise his readers, I would suggest that, after finishing the first essay, they should (if they retain a stomach for more) proceed at once to the last. This done, they will find the others all in a sense lesser variations (if I may change my metaphor) upon the same themes.

In spite, however, of the diversity of their occasions, there is a common thread running through them, a common background of ideas. I do not know whether I am justified in calling those ideas especially biological, but they are certainly ideas which must present themselves to any biologist who does not deliberately confine himself to the technicalities of his science.

The biologist cannot fail to be impressed by the fact that his science to-day is, roughly and broadly speaking, in the position which Chemistry and Physics occupied a century ago. It is beginning to reach down from observation to experimental analysis, and from experimental analysis to grasp of principle. Furthermore, as the grasp of principles in physicochemical science led speedily to an immense new extension both of knowledge and of control, so it is not to be doubted that like effects will spring from like causes in biology. But whereas the extension of control in physics and chemistry led to a multiplication of the number of things which man could do and experience, the extension of control in biology will *inter alia* mean an alteration of the modes of man's experience itself. The one, that is to say, remained in essence a quantitative change so far as concerns the real life of man; the other can be a qualitative change. Applied physics and chemistry bring more grist to the mill; applied biology will also be capable of changing the mill itself.

The possibilities of physiological improvement, of the better combination of existing psychical faculties, of the education of old faculties to new heights, and of the discovery of new faculties altogether—all this is no utopian silliness, but is bound to come about if science continues her current progress.

Take but one example. In the first half of last

century, hypnotism, or mesmerism as it was then called, was in complete scientific disrepute. To-day, all the main claims of its founders have been verified, and many new facts unearthed. Every text-book on the subject will tell you that men may be made insensible to pain by hypnosis alone without any drug, many women even being delivered of children under its influence without suffering. Temperature can be changed, blisters raised, and many other processes not normally under the control of the will can similarly be affected. The mind can be raised to an abnormal sensitiveness, in which differences between objects that are completely unrecognizable in ordinary waking existence, such as those between the backs of two cards in a pack, may be easily distinguished.

If such possibilities are open to the empiricism of the hypnotist, what may we not await from any truly scientific knowledge of mind, comparable even in low degree to our knowledge of, say, electricity?

But these in a sense are all details, relevant in a way, and yet only details. There is something still more fundamental in the biologist's attitude. He has to study evolution, and in that study there is brought home to him, more vividly than to any one to whom the facts are not so familiar, that in spite of all appearances to the contrary there has been, throughout the whole of evolution, and most markedly in the rise of man from his pre-human forbears, a real advance, a progress.

He sees further that the most remarkable single
feature in that progress has been the evolution of
self-consciousness in the development of man. That
has made possible not only innumerable single
changes, but a change in the very method of change
itself; for it substituted the possibility of conscious
control of evolution for the previous mechanism of
the blind chances of variation aided by the equally
blind sifting process of natural selection, a mechanism in which consciousness had no part.

Most of mankind, now as in the past, close their
eyes to this possibility. They seek to put off their
responsibility on to the shoulders of various abstractions which they think can bear their burden well
enough if only they are spelt with a capital letter:
—Fate—God—Nature—Law—Eternal Justice—and
such like. Men are educated to be self-reliant and
enterprising in the details of life, but dependent, unreflective, *laissez-faire* about life itself. The idea that
the basis of living could be really and radically altered is outside most people's orbit; and if it is forced
upon their notice, they as often as not find it in some
way immoral.

Closely connected with this, in a sense its corollary,
we have the fact that ninety-nine people out of a
hundred are concerned with getting a living rather
than with living, and that if for any reason they are
liberated from this necessity, they generally have not
the remotest idea how to employ their time with

either pleasure or profit to themselves or to others.

There are two ways of living: a man may be casual and simply exist, or constructive and deliberately try to do something with his life. The constructive idea implies constructiveness not only about one's own life, but about that of society, and the future possibilities of humanity.

In pre-human evolution, the blind chances of variation and the blind sifting of natural selection have directed the course of evolution and of progress. It is on survival and the production of offspring that the process has hinged; the machinery is in reality blind, but these emerge as its apparent ends or purposes. The realization of ever higher potentialities of living substance has happened, but only as a secondary result and slow by-product of the main process.

In human evolution up till the present, the apparent ends and aims have for the most part and in the bulk of men remained the same; it is only the methods of pursuing them that have changed. True or conscious purpose comes in and aids the unconscious biological forces already at work.

However, to most men at some time, and to some men at most times, these purely biological ends and purposes of life become altogether inadequate. They perceive the door opened to a thousand possibilities higher than this, all demanding to be satisfied. The realization of what for want of a better term we can

call spiritual values becomes the true end of life,
superposed on and dominating the previous biological values.

When civilizations and societies are organized so
that their prime purpose is the pursuit of spiritual
values, then life will have passed another critical
point in its evolution; as always, what has gone before is necessary as foundation for what is coming,
and the biological conditions must be fulfilled before
the new and higher edifice can be built; but, as when
the mammals superseded the reptiles, so this change
of aim will mean the rise of a new type to be the
dominant and highest form of life.

This can only come about so far as man consciously
attempts to make it come about. His evolution up
to the present can be summed up in one sentence—
that through his coming to possess reason, life in his
person has become self-conscious, and evolution is
handed over to him as trustee and director. "Nature" will no longer do the work unaided. Nature
—if by that we mean blind and non-conscious forces
—has, marvellously, produced man and consciousness; they must carry on the task to new results
which she alone can never reach.

Mr. Trotter, in his delightful book on the Herd-
instinct, draws a distinction between the stable-
minded or resistive and the unstable-minded or
adaptive, and points out how the destinies of society
have usually been entrusted to the former—whence
spring our persecutions of prophets and our neglect
of innovating genius. This will continue so long as

Biblical creation only answer that has stood test of time

My Answer
Billy Graham
Evangelistic Assn.

From the writings of the Rev. Billy Graham

Q: Why does it matter whether people believe in evolution over Biblical creation?
— E.B.

A: The entire educational system is rampant with evolution. Universities that were founded upon Scripture now teach atheistic or theistic evolution, producing skeptics, agnostics or atheists with little or no regard for God. Biblical creation is the only answer that has stood the test of time because it is founded on the absolute truth of God's Word that never changes.

This is in contrast to Darwin's book "On the Origin of Species," where more than 800 times he uses expressions as "we infer" and "we may well suppose."

Guided by these flimsy phrases, we are expected to reach the conclusion that man climbed from beasthood and before that, from a single cell, without intervention from God. Upon this frail foundation of supposition and the wild guesses from those who hate the Bible, the theory of evolution was built.

Evolutionists deny a personal Creator and teach that noble man is growing stronger, wiser, and upward every day. Evolutionists deny the fact of sin, teaching instead the "trial and error" method by which man is supposed to make himself better in every way. But man is not growing better or climbing upward. Monkeys are not making men of themselves but, rather, men are making monkeys of themselves. Evolution is in reverse.

Instead of progress in man, there is degeneracy of body, mind and spirit. Higher education teaches the lie that evolution is accomplishing progress and that a new day is about to dawn. A new day will dawn, indeed, when Creator God will send His Son the Lord Jesus Christ back to earth to make all things new. One day every person who has ever lived will face Almighty God. "A new day will dawn on us from above. ... He will give light to those who live in the dark and in death's shadow. He will guide us into the way of peace" (Luke 1:78-80, GW). Prepare your heart and soul by surrendering your life to Him today.

the accepted belief of the majority is that there exists a Providence who has assigned every one his proper place, or even (oddest whim!) ordained the present type of society; so long as they rely more on authority than experience, look to the past more than to the future, to revelation instead of reason, to an arbitrary Governor instead of to a discoverable order.

The general conceptions of the universe which a man or a civilization entertains come in large part to determine his or its actions. There are only two general and embracing conceptions of the sort (though any number which are not general, and fail because they leave out whole tracts of reality): in the fewest possible words, one is scientific, the other unscientific; one tries to use to its fullest extent the intellect with which we have been evolved, the other does not. The thread running through most of these essays is the attempt to discover and apply in certain fields as much as possible of this scientific conception to several different fields of reality.

Of these essays, "Progress" has already appeared in the *Hibbert Journal,* "Biology and Sociology" in the *Monist,* "Ils n'ont que de l'âme" and Philosophic Ants" in the *Cornhill Magazine,* "Rationalism and the Idea of God" in the *Rationalist Press Annual,* and "Religion and Science" in *Science and Civilization,* this year's representative of the annual "Unity" series edited by Mr. F. S Marvin and published by the Oxford University Press. They have all, how-

ever, been considerably revised and enlarged before
appearing in the present volume. I have to thank
the proprietors and publishers for kindly permitting
me to reprint these.

OXFORD,
  April 1923.

CONTENTS

I

PROGRESS, BIOLOGICAL AND OTHER

EVOLUTION: AT THE MIND'S CINEMA

I turn the handle and the story starts:
  Reel after reel is all astronomy,
  Till life, enkindled in a niche of sky,
Leaps on the stage to play a million parts.

Life leaves the slime and through all ocean darts;
  She conquers earth, and raises wings to fly;
  Then spirit blooms, and learns how not to die,—
Nesting beyond the grave in others' hearts.

—I turn the handle: other men like me
Have made the film· and now I sit and look
In quiet, privileged like Divinity
To read the roaring world as in a book.
  If this thy past, where shall thy future climb,
  O Spirit, built of Elements and Time!

Munich, *Jan.* 1923.

PROGRESS, BIOLOGICAL AND OTHER

"Usus et impigrae simul experientia mentis
Paulatim docuit pedetemtim progredientes."
—Lucretius

"As natural selection works solely by and for the good of each being, all corporeal and mental environments will tend to progress towards perfection" —Charles Darwin

"Social progress means the checking of the cosmic process at every step and the substitution for it of another which may be called the ethical process" —T. H. Huxley

"It is probable that what hindered Kant from broaching his theory of progress with as much confidence as Condorcet was his perception that nothing could be decisively affirmed about the course of civilization until the laws of its movement had been discovered. He saw that this was a matter for future scientific investigation." —J. B Bury.

WHAT is the most fundamental need of man? It would be interesting to conduct a plebiscite of such a question, a plebiscite of the same sort that was conducted by one of the French newspapers some years ago, to discover the opinions of its readers as to who was the greatest Frenchman of the century.

When I say the most fundamental need of man, I do not mean those basic needs for food and drink and shelter which he shares with the animals: I mean the most fundamental to him *as man*, as an

3

organism differing from all other organisms in the power of thought, in reflection and self-consciousness. What variety of answers would be given, I dare not guess; but I hazard the belief that the majority, if the suggestion were put before them, would agree that his deepest need was to discover something, some being or power, some force or tendency, which was moulding the destinies of the world—something not himself, greater than himself, with which he yet felt that he could harmonize his nature, in which he could repose his doubts, through faith in which he could achieve confidence and hope.

That need has been felt by all those to whom life has been more than a problem of the unreflective satisfaction of instincts and desires—however pure those instincts, or beautiful those desires; it has been felt by all in whom the problem of existence has been apprehended by intellect and disinterested imagination.

I say all. There may be rare creatures who, secure in strength of body and mind and in unhampered unfolding of their faculties, possess a confidence by which this need is never felt. They are like those whom Wordsworth drew for us in the "Ode to Duty":—

> "There are who ask not if thine eye
> Be on them; who, in love and truth,
> Where no misgiving is, rely
> Upon the genial sense of youth:
> Glad hearts! without reproach or blot;
> Who do thy work and know it not."

But such are rare; or should we say that their type of mind, though not uncommon in the earlier years of life, only by the rarest chance achieves its course without a descent into that vale where the finite human intellect grapples unequally with infinite problems?

The need has been felt in all ages and in all countries; and the answers, the partial satisfactions of the needs which have been found by the mind of men, are correspondingly diverse.

Savages have endowed the objects around them, living and inanimate, with supernatural qualities. At a higher grade of development they have created gods made with hands, visible images of their fears or their desires, by whose worship and service they assuaged the urgent need within their breast. Still later, turning from such crudity, they became servants and worshippers of unseen gods, conceived under the form of persons, but persons transcending human personality, beings in whom was vested the control of man and of the world.

Up to this point there had been an increase of spirituality in the constructions by which human thought satisfied its need, none the less, the ideas underlying the mode of these constructions had not materially altered As Voltaire so pungently put it, man had created God in his own image.

What remains? there remains to search in the external world, to find there if possible a foundation of fact for the belief drawn from the inner world of mind, to test the conceptions of a supreme being or supereminent power against ever more and more touchstones of reality, until the most sceptical shall acknowledge that the final construction represents, with whatever degree of incompleteness, yet not a mere fragment educed to fill a void, however inevitable, to satisfy a longing, however natural, but the summary and essence of a body of verifiable fact, having an existence independent of the wishes or ideals of mankind.

It was the striving after some such certainty that led Matthew Arnold to his famous definition of God as "something, not ourselves, which makes for righteousness." Dissatisfaction with the assertion that belief in a very special and undemonstrable form of Divinity was necessary as an act of faith has, in a large measure, helped the widespread revulsion against orthodox Christianity. It was the need for some external, ascertainable basis for belief which led such different minds as William James and H. G. Wells to approach religion, and in such diverse ways as in the "Varieties of Religious Experience" and in "God the Invisible King." It is this same need which is leading the representatives of Christianity to lay ever greater stress upon the reality and pragmatic value of the religious experience, less and less upon dogmas and creeds.

It will be my attempt in this brief paper to show how the facts of evolutionary biology provide us, in the shape of a verifiable doctrine of progress, with

one of the elements most essential to any such exter-
nally-grounded conception of God, to any construction which shall be able to serve as permanent satisfaction of that deepest need whereof we have spoken.

Any such construction must take account of many
separate parts of reality. In the first place, it must
consider those realities inherent in the mind of man:
his desire for goodness; the sense of value which all
agree is attached to certain experiences of mystics
and to certain religious emotions; his ideals and their
importance for the conduct of life. But in the second place it must consider those realities which are
independent of man and of his mind—the ascertainable body of hard fact, those things which existed before ever he existed, which would exist were he to
disappear, with which he must struggle as best he
may. Lastly, there is the need for intermediation
between the one and the other reality, between the
inner *felt* and the outer *known.*

Mr. Wells,[1] if you remember, erected a new trinitarianism, which in broad outlines corresponded with
this division. With his particular construction, I
do not in many respects agree. But that some form
of trinitarianism is a reasonably natural method of
symbolizing the inevitable tripleness of inner experience, outer fact, and their interrelation is obvious
enough. In the particular trinitarianism of Christianity, the reality apprehended to exist behind the
forces of Nature is called the Father, the upspringing

[1] Wells, '17.

force within the mind of man, especially when it seems to transcend individuality and to overflow into what we designate as the mystical, is called the Holy Ghost, and the activity, personal or vicarious, which mediates between the individual and the rest of the universe, reconciling his incompleteness and his failures with its apparent sternness and inexorableness, is called the Son.

Some men lay more weight on one of these aspects than on the others. I know a clergyman of the Church of England who, on being reproached during a theological argument with failure to pay sufficient respect to the doctrine of God the Father, replied: "I am not interested in God the Father"; and I know intellectually-minded men who wish to reject the validity of all religious experience because their minds are so made that they pay more attention to external fact and because their reason refuses to let them agree with the interpretations of fact propounded by most religious bodies. But, for a properly balanced construction, for the finding of something which shall serve not as the basis of a creed for this or that sect, but of a creed for humanity, of something which instead of dividing shall unite, we need all aspects.

The idea of Progress constitutes, as I hope to show, the most important element in the first part of our construction—that which attempts to synthesize the facts of Nature; and besides, no inconsiderable portion of the third, the interrelation of inner and outer.

Readers of Bury's interesting book on the Idea of

Progress [2] will perhaps, with me, have been surprised at the modernity of that conception. He shows how, in antiquity, the idea was never a dominant one, and further that the adumbrations made of it all lacked some element without which it cannot be styled progress in the sense in which that word is used to-day.

Not indeed till the late Renaissance can we say that the idea of Progress became in any real sense incorporated with the common thought of Western civilization. From then to the present it has suffered many vicissitudes. Starting in the XVIIth century as little more than a consciousness of the superiority of the present over the past, in the XVIIIth it changed to a dogma, its adherents claiming that there existed a "Law of Progress" leading inevitably to the perfectioning of humanity. In the XIXth century the dogma was questioned, and thinkers began to put it to the test—the test of comparing theory with historical fact. A new lease of life, however, was given to the idea of a law of progress by the evolution theory; but finally, of late years, there has been a marked reaction, leading not only to a denial of any such inevitable law, but often to a questioning of the very existence of Progress in any shape or form.

It is the business of the philosopher and of the biologist to see whether this scepticism be justified, and to find out by a more scientific approach how much of the doctrine of Progress is valid. To the

[2] Bury, '20.

layman it would seem inevitable, once the validity
of the evolution theory was granted, to concede the
fact of Progress in some form or another. If we
accept the doctrine of evolution, we are bound to believe that man has arisen from mammals, terrestrial
from aquatic forms, vertebrates from invertebrates,
multicellular from unicellular, and in general the
larger and the more complex from the smaller and
simpler. To the average man it will appear indis-
putable that a man is *higher* than a worm or a polyp,
an insect *higher* than a protozoan, even if he cannot
exactly define in what resides this highness or low-
ness of organic types.

It is, curiously enough, among the professional
biologists that objectors to the notion of biological
progress and to its corollary, the distinction of higher
and lower forms of life, have chiefly been found. I
say curiously enough, and yet to a dispassionate observer it is perhaps not so curious, but only one
further instance of that common human failing, the
inability to see woods because of the trees that compose them.

That is as it may be. Our best course will be to
start by examining some of the chief objections to
the idea of biological progress, in order to see if they
involve errors of thought which we may then avoid.

The most widespread of all the objections raised
may, I think, be fairly put as follows: "The fundamental attribute of living beings is adaptation to
environment. A man is not better adapted to his

environment than the flea which lives upon him as a parasite, or than the bacillus which kills him, nor is a bird better adapted to air than a jelly-fish to water; therefore we have no right to speak of one as higher than the other, or to regard the transition from one type to another as involving progress."

A second class of objector is prepared to admit that there has been an increase of complexity, an increase in the degree of organization during evolution, but refuses to allow that increase of complexity has any value in itself, whether biological or philosophical, and accordingly refuses to dignify this trend towards greater complexity by the name of progress.

Yet a third difficulty is raised by those who ask us to fix our attention on forms of life like Lingula, the lamp-shell, which, though millions of years elapse, do not evolve. If there exists a Law of Progress, they say, how is it that such creatures are exempt from its operations?

Finally, a somewhat similar attitude is adopted by those who refuse to grant that evolution can involve progress when it has, as we know, brought about well-nigh innumerable degenerations. Granted, for instance, they would say, that the average Crustacean is in many ways an improvement upon the simple form of life from which we must suppose that it arose, yet we know that within the group of Crustacea there are several lines of descent which have led to the production of parasitic forms—animals in

which the activity and complex organization of
the ancestral type has been sacrificed, and as end-
product we are presented with a hateful being, an almost shapeless mass consisting of little else but over-
developed reproductive organs and mechanisms for
sucking nutriment from its unfortunate host. Such
a result is revealed to us in the Crustacean form Sac-
culina, and is paralleled by countless other examples
in almost every class of animals. The degradation
of parasites and sedentary types is equally a product
of the evolutionary process with the genesis of the
ant, the bird or the human being; how then can we
call the evolutionary process progressive?

These are important objections Can they be
met? In the broadest way they can and must be
met by the only possible method, the method of
Science, which consists in examining facts objec-
tively, and by drawing conclusions not a priori, but
a posteriori. A law of Nature is not (and I wonder
how often this fallacy has been exploded, only to reappear next day)—a law of Nature is not something
revealed, not something absolute, not something imposed on phenomena from without or from above; it
is no more and no less than a summing-up, in generalized form, of our own observations of phenomena;
it is an epitome of fact from which we can draw several conclusions. By beginning in this way from
the very beginning, by examining the basis of our
mode of thinking in natural science, only thus are
we enabled to see at one and the same moment how

to investigate the question of progress on the constructive side, and how to neutralize the force of the objections to the idea.

Questions of fact are simple to deal with. It is indubitable that some forms of life remain stationary and unevolving for secular periods; it is equally indubitable that degeneration is widespread in evolution. These are facts. But we are not therefore called upon to deny the possibility of progress. To do so would be to fall into the error of reasoning which we have already condemned. It remains for us to take these facts into account when examining the totality of facts concerning organic life, and to see whether, in spite of them, we cannot discover a series of other facts, a movement in phenomena, which may still legitimately be called progress. To deny progress because of degeneration is really no more legitimate than to assert that, because each wave runs back after it has broken, therefore the tide can never rise.

Similarly with the first two objections. If the degree of adaptation has not increased during evolution, then it is clear that progress does not consist in increase in adaptation. But it does not follow that progress does not exist; it may quite well consist in an increase of other qualities. So with complexity. Complexity has increased, but increase in complexity is not progress, say the objectors. Granted: but may there not be something else which has increased besides mere complexity?

No; the remedy for all our difficulties, and indeed
the only way in which we can arrive at the *possibility* of saying whether biological progress exists or no,
is to adopt the positive method.

Let us then begin our survey of biological evolution in the endeavour to find whether or no progress
is visible there. To start with, we must be clear
what are the sources of our knowledge on the subject.

Direct observation of progressive evolution has, of
course, not yet been possible in the period—biologically negligible—in which man has directed his attention to the problem; and historical record is also absent. The best available evidence is that of paleontology: here the relative positions of the layers of the
earth's crust enable us to deduce their temporal sequence—and naturally, that of the organisms whose
fossil remains they embalm—with a great deal of
accuracy.[8]

We can scarcely ever observe the direct transition
from the forms of life in an older to those in a
younger stratum, nor can we absolutely prove their
genetic relationship. But in a vast number of cases
it is abundantly clear that the later type of organization is descended from the former—that a group of
forms in the younger stratum had its origin in one or
more species of the group to which the forms in the
older stratum belong. Sometimes, however, as in

[8] This holds good, naturally, for any given spot on the earth's
crust once the contained fossils have been carefully examined
from a number of series of strata, they enable us to correlate the
ages of the members of the different series.

many groups of mammals, the gaps are few and small, the seriation almost complete. In any event we have here evidence which, so far as it goes, is perfectly admissible for the main lines and for many of the smaller branches of evolutionary descent.

Unfortunately, it does not go very far—or, we had better say, it is of restricted application. By the time we find well-preserved fossils in the rocks, the main groups of the animal kingdom and their chief subdivisions had been already differentiated, with the one important exception of the vertebrates; while time, heat, and pressure have so modified the earlier strata as to destroy the fossil forefathers of insects, molluscs, crustacea, and the rest, which they must have contained.

Within the vertebrate stock, then, we can learn a great deal from the semi-direct methods of paleontology: but for the history of the other groups and for their origin and interrelations, we are driven back upon comparative anatomy and embryology, into another field of more circumstantial evidence. When, for instance, we find that the fore-limbs of bat, bird, whale, horse, and man, although so different in function and in detail of structure, are yet built upon the same general plan, and upon a plan wholly different from that of the limbs, say, of a spider or an insect, we must either deny reason and say that this similarity means nothing; or assume that its cause is supernatural, outside the province of science, that it is the expression of some eternal Idea, or some plan of a personal creator (in which case, be it noted, the idea or the plan often appears to our intellect as unreasonable and indeed stupid); or finally that it implies community of origin with later divergence of development. When we are dealing with the smaller sub-divisions of some larger group, this method too gives us information of the same order of accuracy as does paleontology: but when we try to understand the relationships of these larger groups, then we are forced to renounce any claim to detailed knowledge. In broad outline, however, a great deal still remains, and this broad outline we can employ for our valuation of the whole sweep of biological progress, just as we can use the greater accuracy of vertebrate paleontology and comparative morphology to fill in the detail within a restricted field of its operation. From these various evidences, direct and indirect, we can paint for ourselves a picture of the evolution of life which, in spite of inevitable gaps and errors, is in its main features adequate and true.

Let us not be misled by the fact that disputes can and justifiably do arise over details: as Professor Bateson put it recently [4]:—

"If the broad lines do not hold, then we must sink into irrationality or turn to flagrant supernaturalism."

Let us then remind ourselves of some of these broad lines.

[4] Bateson, '22.

We know that there was a time when the earth, hot and fiery, could not have been the abode of life Of the first origins of life we know nothing and guess little. What we can justifiably surmise is that the protoplasm of the original organisms was not yet differentiated into cytoplasm and nucleus, and that sexuality had not yet arisen. The bacteria, however specialized in other ways, are still in this primitive condition.

Later, we can with great probability infer that the independent units into which the stuff of life was subdivided reached a size which, though still minute, was at least not beyond or even close to the limits of microscopic vision; they were further provided with a nucleus, and occasionally underwent sexual fusion. In other words, they showed an organization which we call cellular; they were free-living cells. Such unicellular creatures must have been at one epoch sole inhabitants of the earth, and diverged into the most manifold types of structure and modes of life. Such of them as led an animal as opposed to a plant type of existence would be classified under the Protozoa or unicellular animals.[5]

The colonial habit gives advantages of increased size and greater rapidity of motion, of which many

[5] There is a certain school of biologists who object to describing Protozoa as cells This to others appears pedantic, But, whether or no they are right in the matter of terminology, the fact which I am here emphasizing remains, viz., that Protozoa had to be aggregated before the Metazoa, or many-celled animals, could arise.

Protozoa have availed themselves. A colonial existence once attained, division of labour, at first between the germinal and the somatic, later between
different types of somatic units, will be a further advantage. Such organisms, of which we cannot say
definitely whether they are compound aggregates or
single wholes, would represent the most natural link
between the unicellular Protozoan and the rest of the
animal kingdom, the multicellular forms or Metazoa.
And indeed such organisms exist at the present day
—organisms such as Volvox, Zoothamnium, Protero-
spongia, and Myxidium—as adjuvant and confirma-
tory of our reasonable faith.

The multicellular organisms appear to have originated twice over, by divergent routes. There are
the true Metazoa, to which belong all the higher
types, and the Parazoa or sponges, which have never
passed beyond a very primitive type of structure.
Both start as simple sacs, whose walls are formed
from two primary sheets or layers of cells. Leaving sponges out of account, the Hydroid polyps are
the simplest representative of this grade of structure,
while some of the Jelly-fish and Siphonophores have
attained the utmost limit of its inherent possibilities.

The next great step was the intercalation of a
third primary layer between the other two. The
result of this, the so-called triploblastic type of organization, gives the ground-plan for all subsequent

organizations; and later evolution consists mainly in the evolution of this ground-plan.

In other words, we can now pass from the consideration of the general plan of life's architecture to that of its details. During the next great tract of time, that which was novel in life (for we must not be guilty of a *petitio principii* in yet speaking of "advance" or "progress") was brought about in two main ways—by an increase in the size of organisms, and by an increase in the efficiency of their working.

The simplest Metazoa, such as the polyps, as well as the simplest three-layered forms, such as the free-living flat-worms, are all small, composed of an amount of material comparable with that contained in a single one of our hairs. In every group of Metazoa, increase of size is one of the main features that accompanies specialization, and the more specialized groups possess a higher average size than the less.

A jelly-fish against a polyp; a cuttle-fish against a primitive mollusc; a vertebrate against its chordate ancestor; the giant reptiles of the late secondary period against their forbears; a horse against Phenacodus, man against the earliest primates—over and over again does size increase with the march of time.

Not only this, but when there occurs aggregation of individuals to form units of a higher order, as in bees and ants and termites, and in man himself, there too increase of size in the new units thus produced is one of the most notable features. Is not human history in large measure the history of the increase in size of social units?

But size alone is not enough; there is also a definite improvement of the details of life's mechanism—partly revealed as improvement in the efficiency of the parts themselves, partly in the adjustment of the parts to each other, and their subordination to the needs of the whole.

It is scarcely necessary to detail the improvements in efficiency of different organs during evolution: such are universally familiar. But a few examples will point my moral. The lowest three-layered forms have no circulatory system; this, rendered necessary later by increase of size, shows a gradual differentiation of parts in evolution. The exquisite machinery of our heart is directly descended from a minute pulsating ventral vessel such as that seen in Amphioxus. Protection and support are better cared for in insect than in worm, in mammal than in lamprey. But the most spectacular improvement of function, the most important of all the directional movements in evolution has been that affecting the nervous system and the sense-organs associated with it. Few people who have not gone carefully into the subject realize how imprisoned and windowless are the existences led by lower forms of life.

Even such physically well-organized creatures as Crustacea stand at an amazingly low mental level. The other day I was reading a careful account of experiments on the behaviour of crabs. The method by which the sexes recognize each other is so crude that I am not sure whether it deserves the term recognition at all. Before mating, which takes place immediately after a moult, the female is carried about for some time in the claws of the male. The mature males will attempt to lift up and carry off any members of the same species, male or female: but the only ones which will permit themselves to be thus carried about are females just before moulting. Hence by a general instinct to lift any members of the same species on the part of the males, and on the part of the females an instinct to allow themselves to be lifted when in the physiological condition which precedes moulting, the required end is brought about. But of any mental operation such as is involved in sex-recognition in man or any other mammal, there is no evidence.

Fish, to take another example, possess associative memory; they can learn. But they learn very slowly, and learn only the simplest things The jump from their powers of memory to those of a dog, who can be trained comparatively quickly to carry out complicated tricks, is as great as the further jump from the powers of a dog to those of a man capable of learning a page of print by heart in two or three readings.

The first organs connected with mind to become elaborated are the organs of sense: but such *receptor* organs are useless to their possessor, however elaborate, unless put into relation with proper *effector* organs—organs for action, whether locomotor or secretory. So that the first steps are the elaboration of sense-organs, the increase of efficiency of muscles and glands, and, equally essential, the construction of an improved *"adjustor system,"* whereby the stimulus falling on the sense-organ may be translated into action and into the right kind of action. This adjustor mechanism is the central nervous system. Most of the further history of organisms may be summed up in one phrase—the evolution of adjustor mechanisms.

At first, it is chiefly of importance to be brought into relation with more and more of the happenings of the outer world, to be able to see and hear and feel and smell more and more delicately; and to react upon the outer world more and more efficiently and powerfully, to be able to move and to handle matter more quickly and with finer and finer adjustment.

But unless the adjustor mechanism be improved, this process soon tends to a limit. I may illustrate my meaning by a simple supposition Suppose an organism capable of very little beyond reflexes and instincts and with but a scanty dose of associative power: of what conceivable use to it would be a telescope or a telephone? Man obtains a biological advantage from such accessory sense-organs in that, when thus apprised of events at a distance, he is enabled to plan out courses of action to meet the events which he imagines are going to overtake him. but both planning and imagination are entirely functions of an adjustor mechanism, and without such a mechanism, great enlargement of sensory power would only result in an organism reacting too often and unnecessarily to events in its environment.

There is, in fact, an obvious limit to the perfection which can be attained by receptor and effector organs. Striated muscles, the modelling of the skeleton and joints for speed in a horse or greyhound, the eye and ear of higher vertebrates, the mammalian sense of smell—no doubt it would be possible for life to have produced more perfect and more efficient mechanisms—but not, apparently, mechanisms *much* more perfect or *much* more efficient. They stand near the limit of biological efficiency.

There thus comes a time when it is impossible or extremely difficult to give an organism advantage in the struggle by improving its sense-organs or its locomotor system, or indeed any of its general physical construction, whereas it is still possible to confer the most important advantages upon it by means of improvements in the adjustor mechanism, improvements which involve and imply improvements of mind.

This stage was reached by mammals and birds quite early in the Tertiary period; and one of the most striking spectacles of biology, revealed in the fossils of successive strata, is to see Mind coming into its own after this epoch. Over and over again a group of animals is seen to appear and spread, only to be extinguished and replaced by another type which to all outward appearance is similar, no better adapted to the conditions of life. But the two types differ in one point: the later possessed a larger brain, and so, from all analogy, a better mind. Or, to take another example, man differs from the lower animals in no notable *physical* specialization except the upright posture.

After this critical point in the evolution of organisms was reached, further development has consisted chiefly in the development of mind: and this has meant, from the objective, purely biological standpoint, the possibility of summing-up ever more and more power and fine adjustment of response in the present, in the single act.[6]

The first main function of the improved adjustor mechanism was to make ever more complicated actions possible; but this again tended speedily to a limit. The next step was to make it possible for the past to act in the present. Through associative memory, present behaviour is modified by past experience. What this has meant to organisms can be realized if we reflect that certain terms which can justly be applied to a mammal or a bird have no real meaning if applied to lower forms. If we speak of a cunning wolf or a wary crow, we imply that their life has taught them new qualities; but it is nonsense to talk of a cunning crab, and, though we might properly ascribe wariness to a trout, I would not like to speak of a wary Amoeba. In the same

[6] See Lloyd Morgan, '20; Washburn, '13; Köhler, '21.

way we can justifiably say that one dog is affection-
ate, another intelligent: but to speak of an affec-
tionate earthworm or an intelligent snail has no
more proper significance than it would be to say that
a dog was intellectual or religious.

Quickness of learning then became of importance;
but so long as the faculty of generalizing is absent,
associative memory, although liberating organisms
from the prison of a fixed and inherited mental constitution, still pins them down to the accidental and
the particular, an organism can only learn to react
to those particular experiences which chance has decreed that it should have had.

The next and last salient step in evolution was a
double one. Which of its two parts came first is
hard to say; probably they acted reciprocally
throughout. This step was, on the one hand, the
attainment of the power of generalization—of reason, concept-formation, or what you will—and on
the other the origin of tradition, which in its turn
was made possible by the acquisition of speech and
of a gregarious mode of life. By these means, the
human species and its evolving ancestors were gradually enabled, first, to free experience ever more
and more from the accidental and to store what was
essential; and, secondly, to bring gradually more and
more of the experience of the whole race to bear upon
the present problem, and to plan further and further
ahead, and on a larger and larger scale.

This has meant, among other things, that for the

first time in biological history there has been an
aggregation (in the technical biological sense) of
minds. Over and over again in evolution does the
process of aggregation appear.[7] It is an advantage,
for at one jump it lands life on a new level of size,
with new possibilities of division of labour and specialization. It appears in the aggregation of Protozoa to form the colonial ancestor of all higher,
many-celled forms. It appears again on this new
level in the aggregation of hydroid polyps, of poly-
zoa, of ascidians, and especially in the beautiful floating Siphonophora, in which the polyp-like units
(themselves historically aggregates of cells) have
become so subordinate in relation to the whole that
they can often scarcely be recognized as individuals,
and the individuality of the aggregate is much more
marked than that of its components. It appears in
a new way in the Termites and in the social Hy-
menoptera—ants, bees, and wasps. Here the bonds
uniting the members of the aggregate are not physical but mental, their sense-impressions and instincts;
but the principle is identical throughout. Finally in
man we have not merely aggregation of physical individuals held together by mental bonds, but aggregation of minds as well as of physical individuals.

In many mammals and birds, each generation can
extend its influence on to the next, and the experience of the parents is in part made available to the
offspring. But never until the origin of speech was

[7] Huxley, '12.

it possible for a whole series of generations to be linked together by experience, never could experience be cumulative, never could one mind know what another mind, remote in time, had been thinking or feeling. Biologically, evolution since the time of origin of this new process has consisted essentially in the enlargement and specialization of aggregations of minds, and the improvement of the tradition which constitutes the mode of inheritance for these aggregations—that tradition which, like Hugo's "Nef magique et suprême" of human destiny, will eventually have "fait entrer dans l'homme tant d'azur qu'elle a supprimé les patries."

It will, I hope, have been clear, even from the few examples which I have given, that there has been a main direction in evolution. At the close of the paper I shall try to point out that since motion in this direction has led to the production of an increasing intensity of qualities which we are unanimous in calling valuable, since in other words the application of our scale of values tends in the same direction as has the march of evolutionary history, that therefore we are justified in calling this direction progressive, and indeed logically compelled to give to motion in this direction a name which, like progress, implies the idea of value

I shall therefore, from now on, use the term *biological progress* to denote movement in the direction which we have sketched in outline, and shall shortly proceed to define more accurately. In so doing, I perhaps beg the question, to be proved I hope later, as to whether the observed direction is progressive: but I no longer beg the question of whether evolution is a directional process. However we may argue on the facts, the facts remain· and the facts are that there has been an increase in certain qualities of organisms, both physical and mental, during geological time.

Meanwhile, let it be remembered, the simplest forms have survived side by side with the more complex, the less specialized with the more specialized. Even when we can trace a causal relation between the rise of one group and the decay of another, as with the mammals and birds on the one hand, and the reptiles on the other, even then numbers of the defeated group continue to exist. Thus, in broad terms, evolution is not a transformation, be it progressive or no, of the whole of living matter, but of a part of it.

I will endeavour to sum up, in brief, what seem to me the salient points of that process, a sketch of which, inevitably hasty and inadequate, I have just tried to give.

During the time of life's existence on this planet, there has been an increase, both in the average and far more in the upper level, of certain attributes of living things.

In the first place there has been an increase in their size, brought about by two methods, first by the increase of size of the units of life themselves (cells, metazoan individuals, communities), secondly by their aggregation; and this has been accompanied by a (very roughly) parallel increase in the duration of life.

Next, there has been an increase in their complexity; and this in its turn depends upon the fact that a division of labour has been brought about between the parts of organisms, each part becoming specialized for greater efficiency in the performance of some particular function. In the fewest words, the separate bits of machinery of which organisms are composed have become more efficient.

In the third place, there has been an increase in the harmony of these parts, and consequently in the unity of the whole. Delicate mechanisms for coordination have been developed, and arrangements whereby one portion becomes dominant over the rest, and so a material basis for unification is given.

In the fourth place, there has been an increase of self-regulation. The outer environment changes from month to month, from hour to hour. The more complex products of evolution are in high degree exempt from the consequences of these changes, through being the possessors of a constant internal environment which, beyond the narrowest limits, it is most difficult to alter.

Fifthly, there has been an increase in the possibility of bringing past experience to bear on present problems. At the base is the power of modifying normal reactions with repetition; then come some simple degrees of memory; then associative memory, as in birds and mammals, for whom most reactions are not given in the inherited constitution, but must be learnt; then rational memory, in which the power of generalization liberates life from blind dependence upon the local and the accidental; and finally tradition, whereby the amount of experience available to the developing race is not constituted merely by the isolated and limited experiences of its members, but by their sum. More and more of the past becomes directly operative in the present; further and further into the future can the aim of the present extend.

Finally we can conclude with a high degree of certainty that the psychical faculties—of knowing, feeling, and willing—have increased in intensity, and also in their relative importance for the life of the individual organism.

We have condensed our summary into these six general statements; if we wish to reach a still more general form, the most general form possible, we can redistil it thus: During the course of evolution in time, there has been an increase in the control exerted by organisms over their environment, and in their independence with regard to it; there has been an increase in the harmony of the parts of organisms; and there has been an increase in the psychical powers of organisms, an increase of willing, of feeling, and of knowing

This increase has not been universal; many organisms have remained stationary or have even regressed; many have shown increase in one particular but not in others.   But the *upper level* of these properties of living matter has been continually raised, their average has continually increased.   It is to this increase, continuous during evolutionary time, in the average and especially in the upper level of these properties that, I venture to think, the term biological progress can be properly applied.

Used thus it is no more an a priori or an undefined concept   It is a name for a complicated set of actual phenomena, and if, with progress thus defined, we were to speak of a law of progress in evolution, we should be using the term law in a perfectly legitimate way, as denoting a generalization based on observed facts, and not as pre-supposing any vitalistic principle of perfectibility, any necessary and mysterious tendency of organisms to advance independently of circumstances.

The gas laws state that the pressure of a gas kept at constant volume increases in a particular way with increase of temperature.   Now the pressure of a confined gas depends on the rate at which its particles bombard the walls in which they are contained, and the speed at which they are travelling   In a gas whose temperature is raised, many particles will, at any given moment, be travelling more slowly than the average rate when it was cooler, many even which had been travelling fast may now be travelling slowly.   None the less, the average speed of all the particles is greater; and this and nothing else is what with perfect justification we sum up as our *law*.

In biological evolution, some organisms degenerate, some remain stationary, but the average of certain properties, and more especially their upper level, increases; and this tendency for certain properties to become more marked, this and nothing else, is what we sum up and generalize, again with perfect justification, as the law of biological progress.

The mechanism of biological progress demands a word: for it is noticeable that a mere fact, however well attested, makes a very different kind of impression from a fact explained and brought into relation with the rest of our knowledge. The impression is either less powerful; or else, an explanation being sought for, an erroneous one is found. It was Darwin's great merit that, not content with the piling up of evidence in favour of the reality of Evolution, he at the same time advanced a theory which made it at least possible to understand how Evolution could have come to pass as a natural process. The effect was multiplicative on men's minds, not merely additive, for facts are too bulky to be lugged about conveniently except on wheels of theory.

The fact of biological progress has struck many observers. Some have been content to believe that the single magic formula of "Natural Selection" would explain it adequately and without further trouble, forgetting that there must be at least some points of difference between a natural selection producing a degenerate type and natural selection leading to prog-

gress. Some biologists have lumped it, together
with all other evolutionary processes which seem to
show us a development along predetermined lines,
under the head of *orthogenesis*—the (hypothetical!)
tendency of organisms to unfold just one type of
hidden potentiality. Bergson has been particularly
struck with it: refuses to allow that it can have anything to do with Natural Selection or any determin-
ist process, and ascribes it to his *élan vital*.

Here, as so often elsewhere, Bergson reveals himself as a good poet but a bad scientist. His intellectual vision of evolution as a fact, as something happening, something whole, to be apprehended in a
unitary way—that is unsurpassed. He seems to see
it as vividly as you or I might see a hundred yards
race, holding its different incidents and movements
all in his mind together to form one picture. But he
then goes on to give a symbolic description of what
he sees—and then thinks that his symbols will serve
in place of analytic explanations. There *is* an "urge
of life"; and it is, as a matter of fact, urging life up
the steps of progress. But to say that biological
progress is explained by the *élan vital* is to say that
the movement of a train is "explained" by an *élan
locomotif* of the engine: it is to fall into the error, so
often condemned in scientists by philosophers, and
ridiculed in both by satirists, of hanging or at least
disposing of a difficulty by giving it a long name.

Let us think of the condition of life on earth at
any given moment of her evolution. Certain possi-

bilities have been realized by her—others have not. To take a trenchant example, before the Carboniferous or thereabouts, the vertebrates had not realized their possibilities of terrestrial existence—nearly half the globe's surface lay waiting to be colonized by backboned animals. The earth's surface was conquered then—but the air remained unsubdued before the mid-Secondary. In every period, there must be not only actual gaps unfilled in the economy of nature—such and such an animal is without parasites, such and such a hot spring or salt lake is without tenants; but also improvements can be made in existing types of organization—a tapeworm could be more firmly attached, a salt-lake shrimp could tolerate an even higher concentration of brine.

These two sorts of possibilities really overlap. For instance, an increased efficiency of vision must be an improvement in pre-existing structures and creatures; it also involves the conquest of new regions of environment, and so in a real sense the occupation of a new biological niche.

In any case, the changes which would confer advantage in the struggle for existence may take place in any direction—with, or against, or at right angles to the stream of progress. By means of those which march with that stream, the upper level of life's attainment is raised. But the struggle still goes on: and again, starting from this new condition, there will be variations in every direction which will have survival value, and some of these will be progressive;

and so the upper level will be once more raised.

The process will take time, for, whatever theory of variation we may hold [8]—the old idea of small continuous variations; or that of large mutations big enough to produce new species at one jump; or the most probable theory of numerous small mutations —they one and all must grant that the largest variation occurring at one time in a living species is infinitesimal in comparison with the secular changes of evolution.

There will further be a premium upon progressive changes, since a progressive change will generally land its possessor in virgin soil, so to speak; if not in an actually new physical environment, then in a biologically new situation. The placental mammal occupies the same dry land as did the wonderful reptilian types of the Secondary epoch. But constant temperature and embryonic nutrition within its mother provide delicately adjusted conditions in the early phases of development which in their turn enabled a more elaborate and more delicately responding brain machinery to be constructed in development, and so advanced their possessors on to new shores of control and independence.

There will thus be a constant biological pressure (to use a term which, though still symbolic, a mere analogy, is less misleading and question-begging than *élan vital*) tending to push some of life on to new levels of attainment, new steps in progress, *because*

[8] See Babcock and Clausen, '19.

any variations in that direction will have selection value, a selection value above the ordinary. And the process will be a gradual one, because variations are not very large; so that life no more realizes all potentialities of progress at once than did the United States or any other new country receive a uniform population over all its extent as soon as it was discovered, but had its people move in from the coasts in a regular and orderly advance.

There are plenty of parallels from human affairs. Indeed, the evolutionist can often gain valuable light on his subject, on what one may call the economics of the process, by turning to study the development of human inventions and machines. There, although the ways in which variations arise, and the way they are transmitted, are different from those of organic evolution, yet the type of "pressure," the perpetual struggle, and the advantage of certain kinds of variation therein—these are in essence really similar.

What could be more striking than the parallel between the rise of the mammals to dominance over the reptiles, and the rise of the motor vehicle to dominance over that drawn by horses?

In both cases, a comparatively long period in which the new type is in a precarious and experimental stage, only just managing to exist, of small size and rare occurrence, and in no real sense a serious rival to its old-established competitors. Then, suddenly, a change. It reaches a level at which it can effectively compete with them. What happens? In the

case both of man-made machine and evolving vertebrate group, there is first a sudden increase in numbers of the new, a corresponding decrease in numbers
of the old type. The upper level of size of the new
type also begins to increase, and it begins to split up
into a great number of differentiated sub-types.
Some of these sub-types become extinct, others, on
the other hand, are gradually improved, while still
others undergo such rapid change as to merit the
style of new sub-types. The upper level of size,
complexity, and efficiency increase, both in animal
and machine.

It is as well to remember that survival-value means
only what it says. A variation with survival-value
helps its possessors to survive. it is not the best possible variation of the kind. In the developing motor-
car, the substitution of four for one or two cylinders
was a great improvement. It had "survival-value";
and not until the majority of cars came to be four-
cylindered was the additional advantage of six or
eight cylinders large enough to bring them into existence as dominant types.

To the interrelated evolution of carnivore and
herbivore, again, leading to increase of size and speed
in both, of wariness in one, of tooth and claw in the
other, we have again a close parallel in the interrelated evolution of armour-plating and of projectiles.
Here again the process is gradual. We can further
see that the sudden "development" of full modern
armour on the first iron-clad would have been ac-

tually disadvantageous, since it would have reduced its speed relatively to other less heavily protected ships, without conferring any corresponding benefit in the way of defence against the comparatively inefficient projectiles of the day. Only when the range and piercing power of the projectiles increased did increase of armour become imperative.

To resume our pressure analogy, the natural increase of all organisms leads to a "biological pressure." So long as a species remains unchanged, so long must it stay subjected to the full force of this pressure. But if it changes in such a way that it can occupy a new niche in environment, it is expanding into a vacuum or a region of lower pressure. Natural increase soon fills this up to the same level of pressure, and conditions thus become favourable for expansion into new low-pressure areas previously out of reach of the normal range of variation. Variation towards such "low-pressure" regions may be progressive, retrogressive, or neutral: but it is obvious that at each stage of evolution there will always be a low-pressure fringe, representing a considerable fraction of the "low-pressure" area within the range of variability, the occupation of which would be biologically progressive.

Thus from the well-established biological premisses of (1) the tendency to geometrical increase with consequent struggle for existence, (2) some form of inherited variability, we can deduce as necessary consequence, not only the familiar but none the less fundamental fact of Natural Selection, but also the almost neglected fact that a *certain fraction* of the guiding force of Natural Selection will inevitably be pushing organisms into changes that are progressive.

This will of course be true only so far as the general conditions of the environment remain within certain limits: it is probable that too great reductions of temperature or moisture on the surface of the earth would lead to a gradual reversal of progress before the final extinction of life. Up to the present, however, it is clear that such conditions have not occurred, or, possibly, have occurred only for short periods. The general state has been one in which steady, slow progress has been achieved. Progress, like adaptation, is in pre-human evolution almost entirely the resultant of blind chance and blind necessity.

What corollaries and conclusions may be drawn from the establishment of the fact of biological progress? In the first place, it permits us to treat human progress as a special case of a more general process Biologically speaking, the human species is young—not perhaps still in infancy, but certainly not yet attained to any stable maturity. The conception, common enough in much traditional thought, that man as a species is old, far removed from all pristine vigour and power, is demonstrably untrue. The genus Homo has not yet adapted itself to the new conditions and the new possibilities arising out of the acquisition of reason and tradition. Its his-

tory so far is a record of experiment after experiment.
From a period so short and so empirical it is impossible to deduce any general law of progress. In certain respects, as we shall see more in detail later,
there has been advance; in others, the species has
been stationary. But whether humanity in this or
that particular has progressed is for the moment comparatively immaterial. Humanity is part of life, a
product of life's movement; and in life as a whole
there is progress.[9]

What is more, there was progress before man ever
appeared on the earth, and its reality would have
been in no way impaired even if he had never come
into being. His rise only continued, modified, and
accelerated a process that had been in operation since
the dawn of life.

Here we find, in the intellectual sphere at least,
that assurance which men have been seeking from
the first. We see revealed, in the fact of evolutionary progress, that the forces of nature conspire together to produce results which have value in our
eyes, that man has no right to feel helpless or without support in a cold and meaningless cosmos, to believe that he must face and fight forces which are
definitively hostile. Although he must attack the
problems of existence in a new way, yet his face is
set in the same direction as the main tide of evolving
life, and his highest destiny, the end towards which
he has so long perceived that he must strive, is to

[9] See Conklin, '22.

extend to new possibilities the process with which, for all these millions of years, nature has already been busy, to introduce less and less wasteful methods, to accelerate by means of his consciousness what in the past has been the work of blind unconscious forces. "In la sua volontade è nostra pace."

For this is one of the most remarkable facts of evolution—that consciousness, until a very late period, has played in it a negligible part. Indeed the rise of consciousness to become a factor of importance in evolution has been one of the most notable single items of progress. Darwin gave the death-blow to teleology by showing that apparently purposive structures could arise by means of a non-purposive mechanism. "Purpose" is a term invented to denote a particular operation of the human mind, and should only be used where a psychological basis may reasonably be postulated. On the other hand, a result can be attained by conscious purpose without the waste of time and of living material needed by the indirect method of natural selection; and thus the substitution of purposed for unpurposed progress is itself a step in progress.

As another corollary of our concept of progress, it follows that we can and should consider, not only the direction of any evolutionary process, but also its rate.

An evolutionary process, if it is to be considered progressive, must have a component in one particular direction—a direction which we have already defined. But this is not all; for even if it be moving in the right direction, and yet be moving extremely slowly, it may, if it have any interaction with a much more rapid progressive movement, actually exert a drag on this; its relative motion—relative to the main current of progress—will be backwards, and we may have to class it as the reverse of progressive. For example, the interaction of carnivore and herbi-vore, pursuer and pursued, led during the develop-ment of the vertebrates to the evolution of much that was good—speed, strength, alertness, and acuity of sense—and of many noble types of living things. But with the advent of man, different methods have been introduced, new modes of competition and ad-vance; and the tiger and the wolf not only cease to be agents of progress in its new form, but definitely stand in its way and must be stamped out, or at least reduced to a condition in which they can no longer interfere as active agents in evolution.

Some such considerations as these will help per-haps to resolve various difficulties of ethics—how, for instance, that which seems good to me may seem evil to another. Even the good, if it be a drag on the better, is evil. Expressed thus, the proposition is a paradox; but expressed in terms of direction and rela-tive speed, it is at once intelligible.

But the test of any such general biological theory as I have outlined will be its application to human problems. And here too, I venture to say, the value of biological method is apparent.   What we ask, and rightly ask, is whether in the laws of biological progress we can find any principle which we can apply directly to guide us in devising methods for human progress.

I do not propose to follow the example of many rather hasty philosophers and biologists, who have thought that, whenever the study of lower organisms permitted the promulgation of a biological law, such law can be lifted bodily from its context and be applied without modification to human affairs   Man is an organism—but a very exceptional and peculiar organism.   Any biological law which epitomizes only facts about the lower creatures is not a general biological law, for general biological laws must take account not only of plants and animals, but of man as well.   In practice, however, the simplest method is to frame our biological laws without considering man, and then to see in what way they must be modified if they are to be applied to him.

Man differs biologically from other organisms in the following main ways.   First, he has the power of thinking in concepts; in other words, his power of learning by experience is not always conditioned directly by the accidents of his own life, as is the case with animals endowed only with associative memory, but he can, by reaching the general from the special, attain to the possibility of dealing with many more, and more complicated, eventualities.   Next, by means of speech, writing, and printing, he has developed a new mode of inheritance.[10] Each community, and indeed humanity as a whole, transmits its peculiarities to later ages by means of tradition, using that word in its largest sense. Physical inheritance of the same type as in all higher animals and plants is the necessary basis, but the distinctive characters of any civilization are based on this new tradition-inheritance. Thirdly, the type of mind which has been evolved in man is much more plastic—a much more elastic and flexible mechanism than any tool previously evolved by life for handling the problems of existence. As a consequence of this we have the substitution of general educability for specific instincts. For the power of performing comparatively few actions smoothly and without trouble, there is exchanged the possibility of a vastly increased range of action, but one which has to be learnt. As another consequence, man has come by the power—impossible to any other organism—of leading what is to all intents and purposes a multiple existence. It is for this very reason difficult to fit man into many of the ordinary biological categories. The physical and mental structure and the mode of life of even the highest of the animals are for all practical purposes a fixed quantity. An ant, for all its delicacy of adjustment, is little less than a sentient cog shaped to fit in just one way into the machinery of the community; a dog, for all his power of learning, is tied down and imprisoned within a rigidity and narrow-

[10] See Carr-Saunders, '22.

ness of bodily and mental organization difficult for
us to imagine.

Man passes freely from one aggregation to another.
He can change his nation or his city; he can belong
to a dozen organizations—biologically speaking, can
be aggregated in a dozen different ways—and play
a different part as unit in each.   He can follow one
profession in the morning, another at night, and be a
hobby-horse rider in between.

This plastic mind has endowed him with a new
biological possibility.   He can do what no other organism can—he can be both specialized and generalized at one and the same time.

In biology, the aggregation of units to form units
of higher grade has been always followed by division
of labour among the units; and this division of labour has, in all infrahuman history, been made possible only by an irreversible specialization.[11]   A sol-
dier-ant is a soldier, and there its possibilities end.
It cannot do what the worker or the queen can do.
A muscle-cell, because it has gained the power to
contract, is cut off from other possibilities; it cannot
secrete, or digest, or carry messages.   The aggregate
of nerve-cells which makes the physical basis of mind
is held fixed to its post, incapable of turning to other
functions.

It follows that the units of all such aggregates are
subordinate to the whole—they have lost their independence, and can often no longer be considered as

[11] See Huxley, '12.

individuals at all, except historically. But in man, none of these things hold. A man can for half his day be the merest cog, subordinate in every detail of his action to the needs of the community, but for the other half be himself, a full and complete individuality, making the community serve his own ends and needs For him, aggregation does not mean complete and irreversible subordination; his specialization is reversible, and indeed his potentialities as an individual actually increase with the increased individuality of the aggregate to which he belongs.

Bearing these differences in mind, we may turn to consider how our doctrine of progress helps us in studying humanity.

At the outset we must guard ourselves against the idea that human society has reached any high level of biological individuation. I may perhaps quote from what I have written elsewhere: "If we were to draw a parallel between primitive types of society and some primitive mammal such as a duck-billed platypus, and to compare the course which we hope society will in time accomplish with what has been accomplished in the progress of the mammalian type from a creature resembling the platypus up to man, with what creature should we have to compare the existing state of human communities? I venture to say that we should be flattering ourselves if we were to fix upon the dog."

Then we must remember that Natural Selection in man has fallen chiefly upon groups, not upon individuals, and differences in the nature and organization of human groups are determined chiefly by what we can best sum up as differences of tradition in the widest sense of the term. The later history of mankind, from a period long antedating written records, has been one of the rapid rise and equally rapid extinction, not only of one group-unit after another, but of one type of group-unit after another. It is further obvious at first glance that the group-units, the types of society which are at present dominant, are far from perfect and far from stable, and indeed that they are evolving, with speed of change hitherto unsurpassed, towards new and unknown forms.

When the mammalian type first became dominant on the globe—at the transition between the Secondary and Tertiary periods—a somewhat similar history was passed through. The new type of organization gave its possessors marked advantages over other animal types· but the full potentialities of the mammal (excluding man) were not realized until well over half of the Tertiary period had elapsed, and man was being prepared in the womb of circumstance. The Pliocene sees the triumph of the perfected types of mammal: the preceding Miocene, broadly speaking, sees the first rise of these new types, while the Eocene and Oligocene show us a rapid rise and as rapid extinction of variation upon variation on the original theme.[12]   With man, how-

[12] See Woodward, '98, Osborn, '10.

ever, only the beginnings of a similar process have as yet come to pass.

Further, we must distinguish clearly between the different ways in which progress may be operative in man. In the first place it can appear, as we have just pointed out, in the organization of the communities to which he belongs and on which natural selection seems mainly to act. Secondly, it can appear as a raising of the *average* of certain qualities among the individuals composing those communities. And thirdly, it can appear as a raising of the *upper level* of attainment in those qualities, in the appearance of individuals biologically higher than any that have previously existed.

This last point may be first dealt with. It has often been urged as an argument against the doctrine of progress that we can trace no advance in the capabilities of the individual man throughout history, and it has even been asserted that no such advance has occurred during pre-history. To this latter criticism there is the obvious reply that at some period there was an origin of human from non-human organisms, and that during the period of transition at least (and probably for a considerable time afterward) there naturally must have been a raising of the upper level of attainments, and still more of possibility. The main point at issue, however, is not to be gainsaid. It appears [13] that comparatively early in the evolution of man, there appeared, in some

[13] See Carr-Saunders, '22.

branches of the stock, a type of mental organization which has not yet been improved upon. An individual possessing it is capable, when developing in proper environment (the most important single elements of which are the organization and tradition of the community to which he belongs) of attaining to possibilities which, measured in terms of the potentialities of any previous organism, are wellnigh boundless. He can survey the whole of mankind, penetrate the future with prophecy, bring the gamut of experience within a work of art, discover the laws by which the universe operates. Judged thus, Goethe is no greater and no less great than Leonardo, Shakespeare than Dante or Æschylus, Darwin than Pasteur, Kant than Plato. ˙

The best type of human mind operating to the best advantage, is introduced to possibilities so vast in comparison with its paltry span of existence that it can never realize more than a fraction of them. Furthermore, since the incidence of natural selection has fallen, from long before historical time, upon the community and its traditions far more than upon the individual, and since the conditions under which the possibilities of the individual can be even qualitatively realized have been rarely forthcoming, it is not surprising that the level of possibility itself has not been raised. Indeed, only too often there has been reversed selection, and the exceptional man has suffered from his exceptional endowments.

There is no theoretical objection whatever to the

idea that new types of mind, new modes of thought, new levels of attainment, could be reached by life: the mental difference between low types of men and men of genius is almost as great as that between man and ape. The difference in practical intelligence between a hen, a dog, a chimpanzee, and a man is largely a difference in the complexity of the situations which can be grasped as a whole so that the right way out is adopted as the result of this unitary comprehension.[14] There is no reason to doubt that other types of mental mechanism are possible which would make our grasp of complex situations appear pitiful and hen-like in its limitations, which would enable their possessors to *see* and solve in a flash where we can only grope and guess or at best calculate laboriously and step by step. But this will not take place, first until the community-environment is made as favourable as possible for such development, and secondly until there is begun a deliberate biological encouragement of new possibilities of intuition, say, or of communication between mind and mind.

As regards the second point, the raising of the average as opposed to the upper level of attainment, not much need be said. That part of our civilization which can be thought of as progressive is largely concerned with this very thing—with making it possible for men to realize in larger measure their inherent possibilities. Further, in so far as there exists

[14] See Köhler, '21.

selection within the community, it largely, under present conditions, encourages qualities such as intelligence and initiative, which are biologically progressive.   And finally, when Eugenics shall become practical politics, its action, so far as we can see, will be at first entirely devoted to this raising of the average, by altering the proportion of good and bad stock, and if possible eliminating the lowest strata, in a genetically mixed population.[15]

Since, however, the main stress in human evolution has been upon the community and upon tradition, it is here that we shall expect to find most definite evidences of progress, and it is here that we do in fact find them.

We have in the first place the increase of the size of units, familiar to us already in lower forms.   This, however, is tending to a limit, which will be attained when the present competition of sovereign states has been replaced (as, if we can read the future from the past, it inevitably will be) by some form of federation covering the globe.   We find an immense increase of control over environment—a theme so hackneyed as to need no labouring   We find an almost equally striking, if less spectacular, increase in independence.   Man becomes less and less at the mercy of the forces of nature and of other organisms, attains much more to self-regulation.   This has depended upon increased efficiency of "organs"—here the extra-organismal organs we call tools and ma-

15 See Whetham, '21; Castle, '12.

chines; and upon increased rapidity and certainty of communication both within and between units. There has been an almost overwhelming increase (displaying too not a uniform but an accelerated motion) of knowledge, of the possibilities of acquiring new knowledge, and of what may be called the "group-memory"—the power of storing and rendering knowledge available, and this in its turn brings about a huge increase in the size of the environment with which man either physically or mentally comes into contact.

As regards increase of harmony or co-ordination, human communities have advanced but little, although in the increase of powers of communication there has been laid the foundation for such possibility.

That this lack of progress is partly due to the extreme rapidity of change in type of unit and of the units' increase in size, is not doubtful, a further ground for it, however, is to be found in the fact that human societies present a new biological problem, in so much as it is impossible, man being what he is, to solve the relationship of individual and community, of smaller and larger unit, in the simple way in which it has always been solved before—by specialization and subordination of the individuals.[16] The early development of codes of law, codes of ritual, and codes of morals represents the first at-

[16] See the second essay of this volume for fuller discussion of this point.

tempt at a solution of the problem: the modern rise of arbitration as a method of settling disputes between whole units and large groups within units is another important step in the same direction. Nevertheless, it is here that the most drastic change of method will have to be brought into being if man's development is to continue progressive.

There is, however, a weighty criticism of the validity of human progress. Granted that human science and invention have made enormous strides, that knowledge has increased and convenience multiplied —is *man*, the living, feeling, personal human being, any the better in essentials for all of this—has it not merely made life more complex at the expense of its depth, more rapid at the expense of its tranquillity and suavity? This is especially obvious in the field of art. It is impossible to maintain that any one of a certain number—a hundred, or perhaps a thousand —of great poets, painters, sculptors, or musicians is greater or has achieved finer things than any other of the number. What is more, in most arts—notably sculpture, painting, and poetry, the possibilities of expression and achievement do not increase, and once a certain pitch of skill is reached, tend to extinguish themselves in technique and virtuosity. When this happens, new ideas generally come upon the scene and work up again from a relatively primitive to a complicated technique along a more or less different path—and so on and so forth *ad infinitum*.

This is not so true of architecture, and still less so

of music. In intellectual matters it is clearly not true of mathematics, where each advance provides the foundation for the solution of more complex problems, nor, similarly, of much of science. But even in this intellectual domain, where the accumulation of knowledge is so evident, where the increasing difficulty and complexity of the problems soluble and solved is so remarkable—even here the individual achievement can scarcely be properly said to increase, certainly not the individual merit or the individual satisfaction. Newton's achievement was no less splendid because to-day any fourth-rate mathematician can use the calculus, nor Euclid's for that his discoveries can be explained to every schoolboy; while for Harvey to discover the circulation of the blood or for Dalton to demonstrate the particulate nature of matter was certainly no slighter task than that needed to show the reality of internal secretion or to discover the infra-atomic world of electrons. The task occupied all their powers, its accomplishment satisfied them; and the powers themselves have not increased—only the ways in which men have learned to use them.

This criticism has been partly dealt with before. We have seen that the present organization of human mind introduces its possessor to a practical infinitude of possibility. We have also seen that there is no theoretical obstacle to be seen at present to an increase of human powers, be it in range of comprehension, intensity of feeling, or brilliance of intuition.

More to our present purpose is the reply that, whereas in all these ways the inherent capabilities have not increased, yet the opportunities of realizing these capabilities have for the bulk of the population increased—in particular, for instance, of gratifying the more complex and the more intellectual emotions, with the multiplication of theatres, of books, of pictures, of concerts. Here, for once, the average has advanced more than the upper level. Whatever overstress and maladjustment the complexity of modern civilization has brought with it, it has certainly made it easier for more men and women to realize more of their potentialities now than a thousand years ago, and far more than a hundred thousand years ago.

There are, then, these facts to set on the credit side of Progress' balance-sheet. It is easy enough to see items on the debit side, and indeed to be so horrifiedly fascinated by it as not to have eyes for anything else. Human history is in one view but a long record of suffering, oppression, and folly. Slavery, torture, religious persecution, war, pestilence and famine, the greed of those who possess power, the dirt and sloth and ignorance of those who do not—the elements of the picture keep on recurring, if not in the old forms, then in new ones. Pain, disease, disappointment, and death are inevitable. Even when a civilization seems to be progressing, there always comes a time when it passes its zenith and topples through decay or defect to ruin. How is it possible to speak of progress when at this present moment there are vast poverty-stricken and slum populations with all the great nations, and when these same great nations have just been engaged in the most appalling war in history?

It is a formidable indictment: but I venture to assert that it can be met by the same argument with which, in the realm of biology, was met the argument from degeneration.

Such facts show at once that any idea of inevitable or of universal progress is untenable, the product of an irrational idealism which prefers its own desires to reality. They show further that, up to the present, suffering and pain on the one hand, and on the other degeneration in a certain number of individuals, are as universal and apparently inevitable in human as in animal evolution. But they do not show that some sort of progress may not have occurred—not necessarily the kind of progress that some of us would like, not necessarily as rapid as could be desired, but yet indubitably and solidly Progress. We have seen that in the hundreds of thousands of species which constitute life, that which has been increased most obviously is the upper level of certain qualities—primitive forms have persisted, degenerate forms have arisen side by side with and in spite of the steady improvement in the highest types. This has happened in man also.

The upper level of control and of independence in human group-units, and in a certain number of fortunate individuals, has obviously increased; but there are the slums, there are the drab lives of thousands in great cities, there are poverty, degeneracy, and crime. All that we can say is that to many at least it seems theoretically possible that man should be able to reduce the amount of degeneration, waste, and pain, to increase the changes to be summed up as progressive.

The future Golden Age of Millenniarism is as impossible a notion as the past Golden Age of Mythology, and more demoralizing. Bury, with pardonable sarcasm, speaks of the result hoped for in it as "a menagerie of happy men . . . in which the dynamic character of history disappears." But once we have accepted (as the great majority accept) life as somehow worth living, the belief in progress asserts only (though there is much in that "only") that life may be made more worth living to a larger proportion of people, although effort and failure always will and always must be conditions of its operation. As Goethe said, "Let humanity last as long as it will, there will always be hindrances in its way, and all kinds of distress, to make it develop its powers."

It is important to remember, what we have already noted, that the history of mankind is largely the history of competition between group-units or communities. When rare communities have been able to escape from this race of competition and have deliberately devoted the energy and resources thus set free to better community-regulation and an improvement in the lives of the individuals composing them, then, like Denmark, they have moved rapidly along a path of real progress. Once an efficient federation of communities has come into being, Progress can knock at the door with some chance of being admitted. In general, it is enough for our present purpose to have shown that some modicum of progress has occurred within the species Man; and that some of the characteristics which most saliently mark him off from other organisms—his powers of generalization and his self-consciousness —are in themselves germs, potentialities of great progress in the future, because through them blind biological progress can become economical, foreseeing, and conscious of herself.

There remains for me only one task—to investigate more closely the relation of that fact of evolutionary direction which we have called biological progress, to our ideas of value. What we have found is that there exists a certain general direction of movement in the evolution of living things; towards the increase of certain of their properties. But when we make a further analysis, we find that movement in this direction is movement towards a realization of the things judged by the human mind to have value. It is movement towards an increase of power, of knowledge, of purpose, of emotion, of harmony, of independence. Increases in these faculties combine, once a certain stage in mental development is reached, to mean the embracing of ever larger syntheses by the organism possessing them— practical syntheses, as in business, or exploration, or administration; intellectual, as in philosophy or in the establishment of scientific laws, emotional, as in love or in the passion for nature; artistic, as in a symphony or great drama. These capabilities are greater in man than in the higher animals, in the higher animals than in the lower, more and more windows being closed and powers pruned away as we descend the scale.

It is immaterial whether the human mind comes to have these values *because* they make for progress in evolution, or whether things which make for evolutionary progress become significant *because* they happen to be considered as valuable by human mind, for both are in their degree true. There is an inter-relation which cannot be disentangled, for it is based on the fundamental uniformity and unity of the cosmos. What is important is that the human idea of *value* finds its external counterpart in an actual historical *direction* in phenomena, and that each becomes more important because of the relationship.

Much of what I have written will appear obvious. But if it has been obvious, it will be because I have here attempted to focus attention on some of the corollaries of a single fundamental truth—so obvious that it often escapes notice, but so fundamental that its results cannot but fail to obtrude themselves upon us. I mean the unity of phenomena—not merely the unity of life, put on a firm footing for all time by Darwin, though that is for my purpose the most important, but the unity of living and non-living, demanding a monistic conception of the universe. For the present, the stellar host (possibly, as recent astronomy seems to assert, assembled not in one system but in a multiplicity of universes, floating through space like a shoal of jelly-fishes in a Mediterranean bay)—the stars seem alien from our life, alien or at best neutral. All that links us to them is that we are built of the same stuff, the same elements.

But the last half-century has at least enlarged our view so that we can perceive that we, as living things, are not alien to the rest of life—that we march in the same direction, and that our hostility to and struggles with other organisms are in part but the continuation of the old struggle, in part the expression of the fact that we have acquired new methods for dealing with the problems of existence.

The origin of life itself, and its movement in time—both these are found to face in the same direction as ourselves. St. Paul wrote that all things work together for good. That is an exaggeration: but they work together so that the average level of the good is raised, the potentialities of life are bettered. In every time and every country, men have obscurely felt that, although so much of the world, taken singly, was evil, yet the clash of thing with thing, process with process, the working of the whole, some-how led to good

This feeling is what I believe is clarified and put on a firm intellectual footing by biology. The prob-lems of evil, of pain, of strife, of death, of insuffi-ciency and imperfection—all these and a host of others remain to perplex and burden us. But the fact of progress emerging from pain and battle and imperfection—this is an intellectual prop which can support the distressed and questioning mind, and be incorporated into the common theology of the future.

Dean Inge, in his Romanes Lectures,[17] quotes Disraeli's caustic words, "The European talks of progress because by the aid of a few scientific dis-coveries he has established a society which has mis-taken comfort for civilization," and quotes them with approval. He bitterly criticizes what we may sum up as Millenarianism (although this after all is but a crude and popular aspiration after what the Chris-tian would call the Kingdom of God on earth). And, after exalting Hope as a virtue, closes with the somewhat satirical statement, "It is safe to predict that we shall go on hoping."

He has been so concerned to attack the dogma of inherent and inevitable progress in human affairs that he has denied the fact of progress—whether in-evitable we know not, but indubitable and actual —in biological evolution: and in so doing he has

[17] Inge, '20.

cut off himself and his adherents from one of the ways in which that greatest need of man which we spoke of at the outset can be satisfied, from by far the greatest manifestation in external things of "something, not ourselves, that makes for righteousness."

One word more, and I have done. There remains in some ways the hardest problem of all. The greatest experiences of human life, those in which the mind appears to touch the Absolute and the Infinite—what of their relation to this notion of progress? They are realized in many forms—in love, in intellectual discovery, in art, in religion; but the salient fact about all is that they are felt as of intensest value, and that they seem to leave no more to be desired. Doubtless when we say that at such moment we touch the Infinite or the Absolute we mean only that we touch what is infinite and absolute in comparison with our ordinary selves. None the less, the sense of finality and utter reality attendant on them is difficult to bring into line with our idea of progress.

> "I saw Eternity the other night
> Like a great ring of pure and endless light,
> All calm, as it was bright."

The Dean too has felt this so strongly that he has made it the keystone of his argument. As he says, "Spiritual progress must be within the sphere of a reality which is not itself progressing, or for which in Milton's grand words 'progresses the date-less and irrevoluble circle of its own perfection, join-ing inseparable hands with joy and bliss in over-measure for ever.' "

I would only suggest that for many to attain to such experiences, which in truth seem to constitute the highest satisfaction at present conceivable for men on earth, it is necessary to organize the com-munity and to plan out life in such a way that hu-man beings, released from the unnecessary burdens of hunger, poverty, and strife, are not only free but helped and urged to attain to such Delectable Moun-tains. Spiritual progress is our one ultimate aim; it may be towards the dateless and irrevoluble; but it is inevitably dependent upon progress intellectual, moral, and physical—progress in this changing, re-volving world of dated events.

BIBLIOGRAPHY

(It was felt that the citation of a few works bearing upon the subject-matter of the essays might help those desirous of pursuing the subject further; but to more than this the lists make no claim.)

Babcock and Clausen, '18. "Genetics in Relation to Agriculture." New York, 1918.
Bateson, '22. "Science" (N.S.) 1922.
Bergson, H., '11. "Creative Evolution." London, 1911.
Bury, J. B., '20. "The Idea of Progress." London, 1920.

Carr-Saunders, A. M., '22. "The Population Problem." Oxford, 1922.

Castle, *et al*, '12. "Genetics and Eugenics." Chicago, 1912.

Conklin, E. G. "Heredity and Environment in the Development of Man." London, 1922.

Darwin, C. "The Origin of Species."

—— —— "The Descent of Man."

Dendy, '14 "Outlines of Evolutionary Biology." London, 1914.

Hobhouse, L. T., '19. "Development and Purpose." London, 1919.

Huxley, J. S., '12. "The Individual in the Animal Kingdom." Cambridge, 1912.

—— T. H. "Evolution and Ethics." Collected Essays, vol. ix. London, 1906.

Inge, W. R., '20. "The Idea of Progress." Romanes Lectures. Oxford, 1920

James, W., '02. "Varieties of Religious Experience." London, 1902.

Köhler, W., '21. 'Intelligenzprüfungen an Menschenaffen." Berlin, 1921.

Lloyd Morgan, C., '20. "Animal Behaviour." London, 1920.

Loeb, J., '18. "Forced Movements, Tropisms, and Animal Conduct." Philadelphia, 1918.

Lull, '17. "Organic Evolution." New York, 1917.

M'Dougall, W., '11. "Body and Mind." London, 1911.

Osborn, H. F., '10. "The Age of Mammals." New York, 1910.

Shipley and MacBride, '20. "Zoology." Cambridge, 1920.

Washburn, M. F., '13. "The Animal Mind." New York, 1913.

Weismann, A., '04. "The Evolution Theory." 2 vols. London, 1904.

Whetham, W. C. D., '12. "Heredity and Society." London, 1912.

Woodward, A. S., '98. "Outlines of Vertebrate Paleontology." Cambridge, 1898.

II

BIOLOGY AND SOCIOLOGY

PROGRESS

The Crab to Cancer junior gave advice:
  "Know what you want, my son, and then proceed
  Directly sideways. God has thus decreed—
Progress is lateral; let that suffice."

Darwinian Tapeworms on the other hand
  Agree that Progress is a loss of brain,
  And all that makes it hard for worms to attain
The true Nirvana—peptic, pure, and grand.

Man too enjoys to omphaloscopize.
  Himself as Navel of the Universe
  Oft rivets him—until he asks his Nurse,
Old Nature, for the truth; and she replies:
"Look back, and find support; you march with Life's main stream.
Look on—be proud; her future lies within your dream."

LONDON, *Feb.* 1923.

BIOLOGY AND SOCIOLOGY

"Come out into the light of things;
Let Nature be your teacher"
—W. WORDSWORTH.

"In matters that really interest him, man cannot support the suspense of judgment which science so often has to enjoin. He is too anxious to feel certain to have time to know. So that we see of the sciences, mathematics appearing first, then astronomy, then physics, then chemistry, then biology, then psychology, then sociology—but always the new field was grudged to the new method, and we still have the denial to sociology of the name of science."—W. TROTTER, *Instincts of the Herd in Peace and War.*

THERE are many facile comparisons to be drawn between the facts of biology and of sociology. The most obvious is that between a whole civilized community and one of the higher animals. Shakespeare employed an age-old fable in Menenius Agrippa's Tale of the Belly and the Members in *Coriolanus*. With Darwin, and the establishment of evolutionary biology on a sound footing, matters took a new turn. Man was now seen to be connected with the rest of life not merely by analogies of his own mind's weaving, but by the living bonds of genetic descent; and it was at once perceived that a more rigid force than had hitherto been suspected might inhere in the comparisons between State and Organism   For, as Spencer argued, was not the State in a true sense an organism—a single biological unit composed of individual human beings just as a metazoan animal was a single biological unit composed, in the first instance, of individual cells?   Further, the investigation of the evolutionary process seemed to reveal certain general laws of its march. beings of the same original constitution, exposed to the environmental forces of the same planet, had reacted in similar ways, developing along parallel lines, and arriving at similar types of organization as end-result.   Thus it might reasonably be supposed that we should find the same general organization and mode of development in one type of organism as in another, in human society as in a vertebrate.

On these bases, Spencer and his followers drew elaborate comparisons of the two, and apparently believed that they were reaching the same degree of accuracy as that found in comparative anatomy when they compared the circulatory system of a mammal with the transport facilities of a State, or drew parallels between the brain and the cabinet.

It was speedily seen, however, that such generalizations were so broad and vague as not to be of much service: that the resemblances were in fact often no more than symbolical or metaphorical, instead of being based upon detailed similarity of constitution or of evolutionary development.   With this, evolutionary theorizing on sociological matters fell somewhat into disrepute. The earlier jubilant certainty gave place to later doubt; and the half-century whose beginnings had roused Haeckel and Herbert Spencer to their imaginative flights closed suitably enough with that remarkable document, T. H. Huxley's Romanes Lecture, in which the greatest protagonist of Darwinism confesses to seeing between man and the rest of the cosmic process, in spite of man's genesis from that same cosmic process, an insuperable and essential opposition, a difference of aim or direction which had turned the original bridge into a barrier [1]

As a result, not only did the particular comparison between society and an organism fall into disrepute, but also all attempts to draw far-reaching conclusions from biology to human affairs.

But the original contention still remains, and is logically unassailable. Man is an organism descended from lower organisms; his communities are composed of units bound together for mutual good in a division of labour in the same way as are the cells of a metazoan: he can no more escape the effects of his terrestrial environment than can other organisms. There *is* therefore reason to suppose that the processes of evolution in man and man's societies on the one hand, and in lower organisms on the other,

[1] For a remarkable critical history of biological thought during this period, see Radl, '09.

must have something important and indeed fundamental in common, something which if we could but
unravel would help us in the study of both.

The correlation of biology with sociology is important not only in itself, but also as part of a more
general correlation of all the sciences. The correlation of the sciences is of particular importance to-day
for a double set of reasons. The rise of evolutionary biology and of modern psychology have not
only changed our outlook on specially human problems, but have altered the whole balance, if I may
so put it, of science. There was a time when the
basic studies of physics and chemistry seemed not
only basic but somehow more essentially scientific
than the sciences dealing with life. Distinctions
were drawn between the experimental and the obser-
vational sciences—often half-consciously implying a
distinction between accurate, scientific, self-respecting
sciences and blundering, hit-or-miss, tolerated bodies
of knowledge. Biological phenomena are now, however, seen to be every whit as susceptible of accurate
and experimental analysis; and indeed to present so
many problems to the physicist and chemist that in
fifty years or so, I venture to prophesy, the wise
virgins in those basic sciences will be those who have
laid in a store of biological oil.

But the main point is this—the study of evolution, of animal behaviour and of human psychology
makes it clear that in the higher forms of animals at
least we are dealing with a category not touched on

at all by the physicist and chemist—the category of mind and mental process. Sir Charles Sherrington, with admirable lucidity, drew for us, in his recent address to the British Association, the problem of the relation between mind and matter as it presents itself to the biologist.

The great change that has come over science in the last half century, or so it seems to me, is the recognition that mind is not to be explained away as a mere epiphenomenon, but is to be studied as a phenomenon. From this point of view, biology will always be the connecting link between physico-chemical science on the one hand, and psychology on the other. There is every reason to suppose and no reason to doubt that life, which we know to be composed of the same material elements and to work by the same energy as non-living matter, actually arose from it during the evolution of this planet. There is, in the behaviour of the lower organisms, nothing which by itself would make us postulate mind: but in the higher insects, molluscs, and verte-brates, the last in particular, mental process is not only clearly present, but clearly of great biological importance; and finally the mind of man, according to innumerable converging lines of evidence, has evolved from the mind of some non-human mammal.

The principle of continuity makes us postulate that this new category of phenomena has not sprung up during the course of evolution absolutely *de novo*, but that it is in some sense universally present in

all phenomena. It is merely that we have not yet
found a method for the direct detection of mental
processes as we have, say, for electrical processes;
but something of the same general nature, the same
category as mind must, if we wish to preserve our
scientific sanity, our belief in the orderliness of the
world, be present in lower organisms and in the lifeless matter from which they originally sprang

In the present state of our knowledge, the study
of physics and chemistry can be pursued without
any reference to mental processes. But the study
of biology cannot: and that is one reason why the
centre of gravity of science as a whole is shifting—
it is shifting for exactly the same reason that the
centre of gravity of a house shifts during its construction—because the foundations have to be built
first.

Our second reason is as follows. Biology is once
more the link between root and flower, between
physics and chemistry and human affairs, in regard
to evolution I say evolution: it would be better to
broaden the idea by saying the directional processes
to be seen in the universe. So far as a main direction is to be observed in physics and chemistry, it is,
as all authorities are agreed, towards the degradation
of energy and a final state in which not only life but
all activity whatsoever will be reduced to nothing,
all the waters of energy run down into a single dead
level of moveless ocean. Biology, on the other
hand, presents us with the spectacle of an evolution

in which the main direction is the raising of the maximum level of certain qualities of living beings, such as efficiency of organs, co-ordination, size, accuracy and range of senses, capacity for knowledge, memory and educability, emotional intensity,—qualities which in one way or another lead to a more efficient control by the organism over the external world, and to its greater independence.

A direction towards more mind is visible; and this development of greater mental powers has been in all the later stages the chief instrument of acquiring control and independence. More and more of matter is embodied in living organisms, more and more becomes subservient to life.

Thus, while in physics and chemistry we see a tendency towards the extinction of life and activity, in biology we see a tendency towards more life and more activity; and this latter tendency is accompanied and largely made possible by the evolution of greater intensity of mental process—of something, that is to say, of which we cannot as yet take account in physics and chemistry.

The biologist may well ask himself the question —"Is it not possible that this evolving mind, of whose achievements on its new level in man we are only seeing the beginning, may continue to find more and more ways of subordinating the inorganic to itself, and that it may eventually retard or even prevent the attainment of this complete degradation of energy prophesied by physico-chemical science?

Is it not possible that this great generalization only applies to phenomena in their purely material aspect, and that when we learn to detect and measure the mental aspects of phenomena we may find reason to modify the universal applicability of this law of degradation?" We do not know the answer to that question: but it is clearly a legitimate and useful question to ask. In any event, we constatate two chief directions in the universe; that seen in biology is in many ways opposed to that seen in physics and chemistry; and both must be taken into account.

I have spent, I fear, a great deal of time on what will appear to many as very irrelevant prolegomena. But the complete breakdown of the older views about nature and man, of the philosophies and theologies based not on observation but on an authority which is no authority, on unverifiable speculation, on superstition, and on what we would like to be so rather than on what happens to be so—the breakdown of all the commonly accepted basis for man's view of himself and the universe, has made it necessary to go back to fundamentals if we are to see where we stand Secondly, the progress of the biological and psychological sciences, as I have already pointed out, has considerably altered the outlook of those who pin their faith to the newer or scientific view of nature, the view which attempts constantly to refer speculations to reality, and to build on foundations which have been tested by experiment.

The orthodox evolutionary view was that phenomena received in some degree an explanation if their origin from simpler phenomena could be demonstrated. As a matter of fact, reflection makes it clear that such an explanation is never complete It is a very incomplete explanation of the properties of water to discover that it is composed of oxygen and hydrogen; or of those of humanity to discover that it is derived from lower forms of life. A precisely similar mistake is made by most psychoanalysts, who consider that an "explanation" of adult psychology is given by tracing in it effects of the events of childhood. In all such cases it is true that analysis is helped, but we are by no means exempted from further study of the later (and more complex) phenomena in and for themselves. Just as adult psychology is qualitatively different in various respects from childish psychology, so is man qualitatively different from lower organisms. Very few attempts have been made to carry over conceptions derived from sociology into biology.[2] But the converse, as we have seen, has often been true, and numerous writers—largely because purely biological are simpler than human phenomena—have been obsessed with the idea that the study of biology as such will teach us principles which can be applied directly and wholesale to human problems.

What we have just been saying shows us the correct path. Through psychology and biology, soci-

[2] Morley Roberts is a recent exception. See his interesting book, *Warfare in the Human Body.*

ology can become attached to the general body cf science; and in so doing it can both receive and give. Since man is but a single species of organism, and, biologically speaking, a very young one; since moreover he presents a peculiar type of organization, it is clear that the broad principles underlying physiology and evolution can best be studied on other organisms and later applied to man. On the other hand, man is the highest existing organism; thus a study of the causes to which he owes his pre-eminence will be important as adding to and crowning the principles derived from non-human biology. Furthermore, not only are man's mental powers on a different level from those of other animals, but psychology can at present make by far its greatest contributions by a study of human mind, so that the psychological side of biology will for the present derive its chief information from man.

Our first affair, therefore, is to see in what important respects man is qualitatively unlike the rest of the organic world; then to investigate what general rules or principles apply equally to him and to the others; and finally to see what corrections, so to speak, must be made before these principles can be applied to the one or to the other.

The qualitative difference between man and other organisms is a cardinal fact with orthodox biology has tended to slur over or to neglect, whereas philosophy has too often tried to magnify it unduly so as to make man frankly incommensurable with his lower relatives, a creature not only unique but disparate.

Man is obviously and undoubtedly an organism of the same general nature as other organisms. He possesses the same general system of organs, working in the same way as a dog, a horse, a bird, a crocodile, or a frog; he passes through the same type of developmental cycle, he is built on the same detailed plan as other mammals; and numerous indications betray his descent from a particular branch of the mammalian stock.

But in his mode of life and type of social organization he is unique. All detailed comparisons between the communities of man and those of bees and ants are as unprofitable in the working-out as they are easy in the making. It is futile to direct the sluggard or any other human being to the ant, since the whole physical and psychical construction of ants is different from that of man, the whole organization of their communities from that of his.

His mode of life is unique because his psychoneural mechanism is built on a new plan, new modes of connection between parts of the brain being associated with new possibilities of mind. Let us briefly run over the biologically most important points in which he differs from the lower organisms.

In the first place, he is capable of speech, and possesses a true language—not a mere repertory of sounds or signs associated with different states of mind, as in some higher organisms, but a language comprising special symbols for particular external objects, and thus making it possible to have a much more detailed knowledge and classification of the outer world. In the second place, he can frame abstract ideas or concepts, and is thus enabled to extract the general kernel from the husk of innumerable separate and different particulars. As a result of these two faculties, he possesses what we may call a new, accessory form of inheritance. True biological inheritance takes place by means of the reproductive cells. In some birds and mammals, the behaviour of the young is modified by what they learn from their parents, so that they profit by the experience of their elders; however, this profiting by experience is not cumulative, but must be repeated afresh in each generation. In man, on the other hand, speech and writing make it possible to construct a continuous tradition, by means of which experience may be actually accumulated from generation to generation. There are thus two forms of inheritance in man, two hereditary streams—biological inheritance, by means of germ-cells or detached portions of the organism, in which favourable mutations may be accumulated by selection, and "experience-inheritance," by means of tradition, in which useful experience may be accumulated by the activity of mind. By means of tradition-inheritance, man is virtually enabled to "inherit acquired characters"; thus the environment in which the latter stages of his development are passed through, and consequently his adult self, the end-product of that development, can be altered far more rapidly than in any other organism. Finally, it is possible, as is being increasingly realized, thus to accumulate experience relating to the alteration of biological inheritance, and so eventually to substitute conscious purpose for blind natural selection in man's future evolution.

Next point: by means of speech, tradition, and invention, man has been enabled to extend his biological environment—in other words, that part of the cosmos with which he stands in relation—till it has reached an enormously greater size than that of any other organism. He is learning ever more facts about the celestial bodies, studying stars that are at an inconceivable distance from him. He is able to travel at will to all parts of the globe. He can penetrate by means of tradition to remote periods of the past: as Mr. Wells has forcibly put it, a modern Englishman can know more of the world in the Classical Epoch than could the most learned Greek or Roman. And even when he can no more get into contact with ideas, he can still unravel facts: flint implements help him to the history of man, fossils to that of life, rocks to that of the globe, stars to that of the solar system. In time, as well as in space, his environment enlarges to a size that is for practical purposes infinite, whereas no other organism can penetrate beyond its own memories, or, at most, do more than profit by those of the generation immediately before it. Professor Keyser,[8] in a suggestive article, has characterized this unique attribute of man by calling him "the time-binder."

Speech and reasoning, with all their consequences, have only been rendered possible through another important qualitative change in the human brain, which in its turn has led to other new potentialities of life being realized in man and in man alone—its flexibility.

In some of the lowest forms of life, such as Paramecium, there are but one or two possible modes of reaction—reactions which it attempts in response to any one of the myriad changes that may occur in the outer world. As we ascend the scale, we find two chief types of alterations: in the first place an increase in the number of hereditarily-given modes of reaction, and in the second an increased power of "learning," of altering behaviour in adjustment to experience. In the insects, the first is chiefly in evidence. Although many insects undoubtedly can profit by experience to a limited degree, yet most of their behaviour is instinctive, in the sense that it unrolls itself automatically and efficiently in the absence of previous experience or of any possible instruction. In the vertebrates, on the other hand, we see as we pass from the lower to the higher groups a definite, steady increase in the power of learning by experience, from the fish that takes weeks to associate a given colour with a given event such as

[8] *Science*, September 1921.

feeding-time, to the dog or monkey capable of learning elaborate tricks after a couple of trials. But even in the most "intelligent" of birds or mammals, the power of image-formation is very probably absent,[4] and the power of concept-formation, of generalizing, certainly so. This fact (quite apart from the absence of tradition, although this too operates in the same direction) means that the associations of animals can only be arbitrary and individual: a rook in one country (to choose a somewhat far-fetched example) may happen to associate danger with fire-arms, one in another with bows and arrows. Life, for the animals, is a cinema, different for each individual, in which one event may be associated with another in the most diverse and haphazard ways. With the advent of the human type of brain, however, experience can be sorted out and properly docketed; the mere cinematographic record is converted into a drama full of significance, the diary into a card-index. By this means, and by tradition, it is possible for man to obtain a much more accurate and more complete grasp of the relationships of the objects that compose the outer world than is possible for any other animal. Through knowledge, as ever, comes power: and as a result, man has been enabled to invent tools and machinery, and so to enlarge enormously his control over his environment. Just as his "range," in the zoogeographical sense, is extended to an unprecedented degree both in

[4] See Thorndike, '11.

space and time, so tools represent, biologically speaking, an extension of himself as an operator. While man is using a tool, he and the tool together constitute but a single unit in the struggle fo· existence. As various writers have put it, tools and machines are temporary organs of man, which have the additional merit of being replaceable if lost or damaged.

But this is not all: the great power of association possessed by man, together with his faculty of generalization and of speech, makes it possible for him to *learn* his rôle in the community, instead of being born with it as are the bee and the ant. Great educability instead of differentiated instinct, infinite possibility, at the expense of the pains of learning, instead of an effortless but limited stock of inborn modes of behaviour—in this again man represents a qualitatively new organic type.

By this means he can escape what has always been a necessity with lower forms: by means of education and machinery he can play a specialized part in the community life, and so build up a community with a high degree of division of labour, without being born specialized. He could not thus learn his rôle if he were not educable, nor if he could not manufacture tools. An ant or a duck or a dog possesses admirable tools for its particular job: but they are living parts of the organism's own body. A worker ant cannot lay down its serviceable carpentering mandibles and become a soldier by picking up a large and warlike pair:—once a worker, always a worker; once a soldier, always a soldier—that is the rule for ants, but not for men

The efficiency and biological success of communities depends on the degree and accuracy of the division of labour and co-ordination between the units of which they are built up. This is true of cell-communities and the second-grade individuals or metazoa or multicellular animals and plants to which they give rise,[5] and also of the communities of metazoa and the third-grade individuals to which they give rise, whether the members of such communities of higher grade are physically bound together, as in a Hydroid or a Portuguese Man-o'-War, or united only by mental bonds, as are the communities of ants and bees and termites As we have seen, the individuals are differentiated structurally for the different functions which they have to perform.

This is not so in human species: a man is not born cross-legged to be a tailor, or broad-thumbed to be a miller, or big-armed to be a blacksmith. Even in the hereditary castes of India, the trade or profession is determined by tradition, and not by inborn structural adaptations.

Still another consequence flows from this educability, this flexible and elastic mental organization. A man can pass from one occupation to another.

[5] See J. S Huxley, '12, for a discussion of the grades of biological individuality.

He can be specialized for several, or combine a high degree of professional skill in one with the generalized knowledge of an amateur in another. It is this obvious but fundamental fact which is at the bottom of many of the failures to apply biological ideas to sociology.

Another human distinction is the increase of the part played by environment in man as opposed to animals (in determining his biologically effective nature). Environment plays not merely a large part, but a preponderating one, in his development after the first year or so of his life. Tradition provides a special environment, made by man for man's own development; and men brought up in markedly different traditions arrive at different end-results just as surely and obviously as do men of markedly different hereditary tendencies arrive at different end-results even though exposed to similar traditions. Traditions are infinitely complex things: there are world traditions, national traditions broad and narrow, class traditions and traditions of profession and trade, traditions of predilection, of art, of religion: and men may be exposed in their development to the combined influence of a number of these. But the nett result of the diversity of tradition is an extraordinary diversity of end-result. *"Nihil humanum alienum a me puto"*—Terence could only say this with truth in the sense that there are certain fundamental emotions and instincts found in all men, and also certain aspects of environment shared by all humanity—the sun and moon, earth, water, and fire, space and time, parents and society, and so on and so forth

I make no apologies for the length of this preliminary analysis, since it is precisely by the neglect of preliminary analysis that most attempts to correlate biology and sociology have failed. The salient fact emerges that with man there has been a radical change in evolutionary method.

As space is limited, I am here only proposing to consider three of the chief contributions which biology can make to sociology—on the idea of progress, on the relation between individual and community, and on the applicability of the doctrine of the struggle for existence to man.

As regards the idea of progress, biology can make a clear and unequivocal contribution: whereas man is biologically so young, his evolution is yet so chaotic and divergently directed, that it is very hard to arrive at definite conclusions from the study of his history alone. It has been a source of constant surprise to me that more use has not been made of biological data in the controversy over this question. In the little book recently edited by Mr. Marvin on various aspects of the concept of Progress, there was no article dealing with biological progress; and even in Professor Bury's notable book, *The Idea of Progress*, biology was as little and as unsatisfactorily drawn upon as in Dean Inge's writings on the subject.

We have already seen that a certain direction obtains in organic evolution. Into the details of this process I have not here the time to go; we must be content with the brief enumeration which has already been given of the qualities of organisms whose maximum level, and to a lesser degree whose average, have increased during evolution.

So far so good. But a process may be going in a definite direction and yet not be satisfactory.

This road leads to London; this other to Puddlington Parva. We all know people who are obviously headed for success, while it is on record that Mr. Mantalini's direction was towards "the demnition bow-wows."

But we know that we ourselves consciously find *value* in things, in objects and aims, in directions and processes. In this we are unique among organisms, and as a matter of fact a large part of our life is determined by the relative values we set on objects. On the whole, however, there is a reasonable amount of agreement among different individuals, at any rate in one country at one epoch, as to what they call good and what they call bad. There are very few western Europeans who find dirt or untruthfulness good, knowledge or bravery bad.

When we look into the trend of biological evolution, we find as a matter of fact that it has operated to produce on the whole what we find good, to bring into being more and more things on which we can set positive value. This is not to say that progress is an inevitable "law of nature," but that it has actually occurred, and that its occurrence provides an external sanction for many of our subjective human hopes and ideals.

True that we are ourselves a product of the evolutionary process and might therefore be thought biased. None the less, it is clear that if a degenerate animal like a tapeworm, or one inevitably specialized like a hermit-crab, could possess and enunciate values, they would be of a very different nature from our own. But we should further find that the direction of the evolutionary process which led to the former was directly opposed to the main trend, that of the latter more or less at right angles to it. The general coincidence of the main observable trend and of our own concepts of value warrants us in calling the one progressive, and in feeling that the other is no mere isolated flicker in an alien or hostile world, but finds a sanction and a resting-place in being part of something vastly bigger than itself. The remarkable and important fact for man is to find, in spite of all the apparently fundamental differences between his organization and his evolutionary methods and those of lower organisms, in spite of the widespread degeneration and "blind-alleyism" to be seen in evolution, that the direction in which he desires to go coincides with the resultant, the main direction of organic evolution. There are no ideals, there is no purpose, in fish or ant or tree: but man's ideals and purposes are the outcome of the blind interplay of forces in which fish and ant and tree play their unwitting rôles. True again that further analysis shows that the methods of evolutionary progress are often crude, wasteful, and slow: that some of our values are unreal or artificial. but this does not destroy the main fact, and only means that each side can here learn something from the other.

The main fact abides—that progress is an evolutionary reality, and that an analysis of the modes of biological progress may often help us in our quest for human progress.

The next great problem on which biology has something to say to sociology is that eternal one of the relation between individual and community. As it is sometimes put, Does the individual exist for the State, or the State for the individual? In all non-human biological aggregates—cell-colonies, second-grade aggregates or metazoan organisms, third-grade aggregates like Siphonophora and insect communities —the very existence of the aggregate as a unit, its biological efficiency and success, depend upon a permanent division of labour between its members, upon their thoroughgoing specialization. This always and inevitably involves a sacrifice of certain of their potentialities to greater efficiency in one of a few actual functions, and in evolution a progressive subordination of the smaller unit to the aggregate.

At first sight, biological principles seem to contradict themselves on this subject. On the one hand, the human individual is, or, we had better say, has the potentiality of being the highest type of organism in existence—far higher, biologically speaking, not only than any human community now in existence, but than any which we could possibly imagine as coming into existence in the future When we remember the general agreement of biological progress with our human values, it is clear that to degrade the individual for the benefit of the community is wrong—a biological crime.

On the other hand, human progress depends and will always depend to an extent scarcely to be overrated upon the proper organization of the community. So long as present competition continues, the very survival of a nation may easily depend upon the efficiency of its organization as a community. Biological as well as human experience makes it perfectly plain that such success, in a unit which is itself an aggregate of smaller units, depends upon the degree of specialization of these constituent units and the division of labour and co-operation between them.

Biology here then lays down that human individuals should become more and more specialized if progress is to continue; but since specialization implies the sacrifice of many potentialities for the good of the whole, this apparently contradicts what we have just inculcated above.

This is where our human flexibility comes in. Man should neither live whole-heartedly for himself, nor throw his individuality, ant-like, beneath the wheels

of the community Juggernaut.   He can escape from
the dilemma by passing from one state to the other.
For part of his time, he can apply his energies as a
specialized unit—for the rest, he can be a complete
individual, realizing the various potentialities of his
many-sided nature, with the community contribut-
ing to his development, not he to the community's.
And not only can he, but he should act thus.

Be it noted, to avoid misapprehension, that I have
here been using the community to denote the single
aggregate unit which from the beginning has played
such an important part biologically in human evolution, not merely as denoting the sum of individuals
considered separately.

Thus biology gives a definite answer to this question too.   Pure individualism is condemned, and so
is what we may call ant-and-bee socialism.   Some
form of the "dual day," to use a current phrase, or at
least of the "dual life," is the method which seems to
be in accord with the enduring principles of biology,
although the precise details are not and cannot be
the biologist's concern, and particular lives, such as
that of the creative artist, who moves on a different
plane of reality, escape his analysis.

I have reserved to the close that biological principle which has been most often and most seriously
misapplied in sociology and politics—the struggle
for existence.   Never was the proverb about the
Devil's quoting Scripture better exemplified than in
this matter.   This fundamental idea of Darwin's has

been used as justification for three totally different
and indeed incompatible political doctrines. In England, it has served chiefly to bolster up *laissez-faire*
individualism and free competition. In Germany
in the years immediately succeeding the publication
of the *Origin of Species,* it was seized upon by the
Socialists as implying equal opportunity for all as
against feudalism or hereditary aristocracy. Later
in the same country (and to a certain extent elsewhere) it was abundantly employed as a theoretical
support for militarism.

As a matter of fact, the use of it as sole principle
governing the interrelation of biological units is
wholly unjustified. As has been shown by a number
of writers, among whom may especially be mentioned Darwin himself, Ritchie in his *Darwinism
and Politics,* and Kropotkin in his *Mutual Aid,*
the struggle for existence is only *one* of two possibilities in this relationship: the other is that of co-
operation, of mutual aid, which is especially well
marked in the building up of higher-grade units from
a multiplicity of smaller lower-grade ones. Two of
the most important steps in the whole evolutionary
process have been based on the co-operation of units
—the origin of multicellular from unicellular organisms, and the development of true man, with his social life, from his pre-human ancestor. It is also
prominent in the lives of many species of the highest groups—insects, mammals, and birds: witness
the ants and bees, the rook, the wild dog, the ele-

phant, the baboon. In fact, once the bodily specialization of units has reached a certain pitch, progress,
as we have seen, is only possible through mental development, and this in the great majority of cases
brings about aggregation into some sort of community, held together by mental bonds.

Besides aggregation of similar units, there has frequently been co-operation between units of unlike
character and origin—witness symbiosis, as in li-
chens; the relation between many insects and flowers;
the formation of flocks consisting of two or more
species, as with jackdaws and rooks, and many other
cases.

Competition and co-operation both occur throughout the whole of evolution: but co-operation comes
to play an ever more considerable part in higher
forms. In lower organisms enormous overproduc-
tion is of no great consequence; their organization is
simple, and, given favourable conditions, they can
turn inorganic matter into their own specific substance at a great rate. But higher forms are more
complex, more delicately balanced, and longer lived.
Accordingly, waste of life is of greater consequence
to them, and methods by which a struggle on the
grand scale can be minimized tend to be more and
more adopted. We find regularly, for instance, a reduction of the number of offspring in higher groups
together with greater parental care.

Thus co-operation, for still fresh reasons, is biologically important for the higher groups. The prob-

lem is becoming increasingly pressing for the human
race, since the time is in sight when the whole habit-
able area of the globe will be colonized, up to a certain level of density and efficiency, by members of
the more advanced races. Biologically speaking, it
is perfectly clear that some co-operative system, involving federation in one form or another, is the
proper system to adopt; and that the "world-state"
—not necessarily organized after the plan of our present highly specialized nationalist-industrialist states,
which appear happily to represent only a temporary
phase of evolution, but none the less an organic reality, a co-operative unit—that the "world-state" is not
merely a figment of unpractical dreamers, but an
obviously desirable aim for humanity. Kant, a century and a half ago even, had seen clearly enough
that some universal society was a necessity for the
unfolding of human possibility, and had gone further
and pointed out that there were indications of a
movement of civilization in that direction. In our
time, this movement has been retarded by the extraordinary and mushroom growth of Nationalism, in which to the average man his "Country"
(really *Nation*) has become his most real God. In
the last hundred years, Nationalism has usurped the
place of Religion as the most important super-indi-
vidual interest of individuals—has indeed in some
sense become a religion. It is leading the world into
an impasse, as do all incomplete and partial conceptions; but, in the Hague Court and the League of

Nations, has already generated the seeds of what will in time devour it.[6]

To sum up, we may say that the crude application to human affairs of the doctrine of the struggle for existence, torn from its biological context, isolated and over-emphasized, is wholly unwarranted. On the other hand, a struggle does continue, both of the direct and indirect type defined by Darwin: and there is no prospect of it ceasing to play an important part in human biology. Co-operation is not, any more than competition, to be taken as the sole desirable principle. Panaceas of this sort do not exist, except to make bubble reputations and quack fortunes. Even within such a highly organized co-operative unit as the mammalian body a struggle continues—the different tissues are in competition with each other for food, and if the available supply diminishes below the necessary level, some tissues will be drawn upon by other more successful competitors, and the struggle will lead to an end-result in which the proportion of the various kinds of cells comes to be very different from what they were in the normal well-nourished body.[7] That is a purely biological example. In man, since the unification of the community is of a low order, it is inevitable that individuals and sections will continue in some form of competition with each other: not only this, how-

[6] See, e g., Wells, '21, pp. 558, 666

[7] See Roux, '81, for a discussion of this important extension of Darwinism.

ever, but the additional fact that man's mental organization reacts strongly to the stimulus of competition make it probable that a "struggle" of some sort will not only be inevitable but up to a point beneficial in any form of society. What is more, once co-operation exists, competition between the co-operative units is necessary to bring out the full efficiency of their combination.

All that the biologist can do is to point out that neither the one-sided application of the principle of struggle nor of that of co-operation is biologically sound. But, as everywhere else in human conduct, after the broad principles have been grasped, success lies always in a delicate, continuous adjustment of conflicting claims, in what one may call a personal conscious effort. Struggle is universal: but by itself it can only lead to a certain stage of evolutionary progress.

The half-baked moralist may lay down the law about right and wrong with the most positive assurance; but, by not paying attention to the necessity for sweet reasonableness, give-and-take, unselfishness, for thought about the thousand and one details of daily conduct, he may be making himself and his wife thoroughly unhappy, ruining his family's chances, and, as a matter of fact, be thoroughly immoral without once suspecting it.

It is in a very similar way that the militarist, for instance, fortifying himself in the doctrine of the struggle for existence with what he regards as an impregnable sanction for his theories, is in reality acting immorally because not attempting to envisage the whole problem.

There is one very interesting evolutionary point which well illustrates the difference between pure biology and pure sociology, and yet emphasizes the natural connection between the two. Once again it has a connection with the greater flexibility of human mind. As we have seen, in the lowest animals behaviour is for the most part unvarying, hereditarily determined: the organism is capable of a number of definite reactions, and if these do not suffice to extricate it from difficulties, it perishes. The first step towards gaining is the power of learning. "Once bitten, twice shy" is applicable to all higher vertebrates; and it is not only the burnt child who dreads the fire (although a study of moths and candles will convince us that "Lepidopteran" cannot be substituted as subject of the proverb).

When, as in the higher mammals, the power of learning by experience is rapid, the individual organism is better able to adjust itself to the dangers of life, and once more there is less sacrifice of individuals in the struggle. The same organism persists: but of two possible types of behaviour, the unmodified innate type is eliminated, the type modified by experience survives. If we like to put it in a way which is perhaps not wholly justifiable, there comes into being, besides the struggle for existence between individuals, a struggle for existence between

The religion of humanism

My Answer
Billy Graham
Evangelistic Assn.

From the writings of the Rev. Billy Graham

Q: It's said that society is selfish and this is why humanism has become so acceptable. Is this something new?
– H.S.

A: Humanism is the worship of man. It has taken on the form of religion; glorifying self and taking God out of His rightful place. A London magazine carried a story that said, "No more subtle enemy has ever faced the Christian church than this one which dethrones her God and replaces Him with its creation."

Young people today may not know who Julian Huxley was, but he said that if humanism is to acquire a wider appeal, it must become a religion. The religion of humanism has been around a very long time, but it's more widely recognized.

Humanism has become for many a polite name for a vocal and aggressive movement against God's truth to advance its own brand of social influence. Humanism isn't new; it emerged in the Garden of Eden – Adam and Eve yielding to Satan's temptation. He told them they could be gods (Genesis 3:5).

Mankind continually rejects the revelation of the Bible concerning the true and living God, substituting gods of its own making. Many intellectuals have come to believe that the human mind can understand everything eventually. This is nothing but total rebellion toward God, and Satan is behind it all.

The Bible warns, "The devil walks about like a roaring lion, seeking whom he may devour. Resist him" (1 Peter 5:8-9). The Lord will help us stand strong in the face of deception if we'll stay in the Word of God and pray that He will give us discerning minds. And always remember to pray for professors and classmates, that God will open their hearts to His truth that never fails.

PEANUTS

BEETLE BAILEY

PICKLES

BABY BLUES

I DO NOT LIKE GREEN EGGS AND | I WILL NOT EAT THEM IN A SUIT. | DON'T

different possible modes of reaction of one and the same organism.

With the advent of man upon the scene, still new possibilities arise. First of all, he is capable of ideas, which, biologically speaking, are to be regarded as potentialities of behaviour. There is no evidence at present that even the highest animals possess ideas or even images.[8] Secondly, these ideas are transmissible by speech and writing, and accordingly tradition has come into being, so that modification of behaviour by experience can be operative not only within the individual life, not only from one generation to the next immediately succeeding, as in many mammals, but for an indefinite period. The experience of Moses, Archimedes, or Charlemagne, of Jesus, Newton, or James Watt is modifying our behaviour to-day.

The result, both for individuals and communities, is that a selection of ideas instead of a selection of organic units can to an ever greater extent take place; and thus the actual extinction of living matter be increasingly avoided. For instance, we find the substitution of judicial procedure, in which the ideas of two disputants about the matter in dispute are weighed and a selection made in favour of one, for various forms of violence and combat in which one or other of the actual disputants was often eliminated. Or again, in struggles between communities,

[8] See Thorndike, *op. cit.*, Washburn, *The Animal Mind.* New York, 1913.

even though warfare is still resorted to, yet it does not operate in the same way as in earlier stages of human evolution. A salient example of this is afforded by the result of the recent war to Germany; although an equally good instance can be seen, for example, in the Boer War. In primitive wars, the defeated tribe was wherever possible exterminated or enslaved· it ceased to exist as an independent unit, and the great majority of its male members were killed. This is impossible under present conditions: and all those who preserve, or have ever possessed, any political sanity aim, for instance, neither at the physical nor the economic destruction or subordination of Germany, but—to use one of those attractive catchwords that sounded so well in war-time—at her "change of heart"—in other words, the extermination, not of a nation, but of a national tradition.

To what extent this substitution of mental for physical will continue it is hard to say; already, to take another field, the multiplication of cheap books has led to an ever increasing number of men and women finding most of their adventure and romance in books instead of in the life that we are accustomed to call real. But that would lead us away from our main point—enough to have indicated another great difference between processes above and below the human level.

There are numerous important questions concerning our right to apply biological ideas of heredity directly to human beings which I would have liked to touch upon. But for one thing I have not the time, and for another, Mr. Carr-Saunders in his recent book on the Population Problem has dealt so fully with the relation between biological inheritance and what may be called tradition-inheritance, that I omit them with a good conscience.

In this brief treatment I have had to ask you to take conclusions on trust, without presenting the evidence on which they are based; this, however, is inevitable when transferring ideas from one science to another. I have attempted to show, first, that biology can profit by incorporating certain conclusions of sociology and so rounding off and completing certain of its own principles: on the other hand, I have put before you my belief that there are certain basic biological principles which must be taken into account by the sociologist—principles which hold good in sociology because man too is an organism.

By now, however, we can see more clearly the way in which the various sciences with which we are concerned, of whose relations we had something to say at the beginning of this essay, properly interlock.

They interlock thus. The physico-chemical sciences are basic to biology. Organisms are made of the same substances as are non-living compounds; their processes are therefore conformable to certain physico-chemical laws, such as the indestructibility of matter, the conservation of energy, and so forth; and in so far as we analyse the material aspect of life, physico-chemical concepts are *adequate*. On the other hand, physico-chemical concepts—or at least our present ones—are not *all-sufficient*. In the first place, the very complicated arrangement of matter which is found in living substance has not been yet sufficiently analysed by physics and chemistry: accordingly we find many processes occurring in biology—such as the directional changes in evolution of which we have spoken—which could not have been foretold on our present physico-chemical knowledge, but must be investigated separately as adding to our store of facts and principles, in the confident hope that a synthesis will one day be possible. Secondly, a whole new category of phenomena, the psychological, is first met with in biology, and to this we cannot as yet apply physical or chemical ideas at all.

For a combination of these two reasons, biology deals with certain concepts which are not implicit in current physico-chemical ideas. Physics and chemistry are basic for biology, but they are not exhaustive.

In a very similar way, biology is basic for sociology, but again not exhaustive. Certain limits are set to human life through man's organic nature. Certain of his activities can be completely analysed in terms of biology. But other of his activities, especially those concerned with his new type of mental organization, find no counterpart in the rest of the biological kingdoms, and must be studied in and for themselves.

Bergson would have us believe that evolution is

creative. It is better to say, with Lloyd Morgan, that it is emergent. With new degrees of complexity, new qualitative differences emerge. Thus the sciences are a hierarchy, the subject-matter of one constituting the foundation for the next in the series. All that biology can do for sociology is to help her to build her foundations solidly and correctly: but we all know that without good foundations no building is safe.

BIBLIOGRAPHY

Bury, J. B., '20. "The Idea of Progress." London, 1920.

Carr-Saunders, A. M., '22. "The Population Problem." Oxford, 1922.

Hobhouse, L. T., '01. "Mind in Evolution." London, 1901.

Huxley, J. S., '12. "The Individual in the Animal Kingdom." Cambridge, 1912.

Keyser, '21. "Science" (N.S.) New York, 1921.

Kropotkin, Prince, '08. "Mutual Aid, A Factor in Evolution." London, 1908.

Lloyd Morgan, C., '23. "Emergent Evolution." London, 1923.

Marvin, F. S. "Progress and History (5th Imp.). Oxford, 1921.

Radl, E., '09. "Geschichte der biologischen Theorien," vol. ii. Leipzig, 1909.

Ritchie, '01. "Darwinism in Politics" (4th Ed.). London, 1901.

Roberts, Morley, '20. "Warfare in the Human Body." London, 1920.

Roux, W., '81. "Der Kampf der Teile im Organismics." 1881.

Sherrington, '22. "The Advancement of Science, 1922." London, 1922.

Spencer, Herbert "First Principles," "Principles of Biology," "Principles of Sociology."

Thorndike, E. L., '11. "Animal Intelligence." New York, 1911.

Trotter, W., '19. "Instincts of the Herd in Peace and War" (2nd Ed.). London, 1919.

Wells, H. G., '21. "The Outline of History." London, 1921.

III

ILS N'ONT QUE DE L'AME: AN ESSAY ON BIRD-MIND

THE BIRDS

To most of us, a bird's a feathered song
  Which for our pleasure gives a voice to spring.
  We make a symbol of its airy wing
Bright with the liberty for which we long.

Or we discover them with love more strong
  As each a separate, individual thing
  Which only learns to act, or move, or sing
In ways that wholly to itself belong.

But some with deeper and more inward sight
  See them a part of that one Life which streams
Slow on, towards more mind—a part more light
  Then we, unburdened with regrets, or dreams,
Or thought   A winged emotion of the sky,
The birds through an eternal Present fly.

OXFORD, *April* 1923.

ILS N'ONT QUE DE L'ÂME:

AN ESSAY ON BIRD-MIND

"O Nightingale, thou surely art
A creature of a fiery heart."
—W. WORDSWORTH.

"The inferior animals, when the conditions of life are favourable, are subject to periodical fits of gladness, affecting them
powerfully and standing out in vivid contrast to their ordinary
temper   . Birds are more subject to this universal joyous instinct than mammals, and . . . as they are much freer than
mammals, more buoyant and graceful in action, more loquacious,
and have voices so much finer, their gladness shows itself in a
greater variety of ways, with more regular and beautiful mo-
tions, and with melody."—W. H. HUDSON

"How do you know but ev'ry Bird that cuts the airy way
Is an immense world of delight, clos'd by your senses five?"
—— BLAKE

"*ILS n'ont pas de cerveau—ils n'ont que de
l'âme.*" A dog was being described, with all
his emotion, his apparent passion to make himself understood, his failure to reach comprehension;
and that was how the French man of letters summed
up the brute creation—"*pas de cerveau—que de
l'âme.*"

Nor is it a paradox: it is a half-truth that is more
than half true—more true at least than its converse,
which many hold.

There is a large school to-day who assert that ani-

107

mals are "mere machines"   Machines they may be:
it is the qualification which does not fit.   I suppose
that by saying "mere" machines it is meant to imply
that they have the soulless, steely quality of a machine which goes when it is set going, stops when another lever is turned, acts only in obedience to outer
stimuli, and is in fact unemotional—a bundle of
operations without any quality meriting the name of
a self.

It is true that the further we push our analysis of
animal behaviour, the more we find it composed of a
series of automatisms, the more we see it rigorously
determined by combination of inner constitution and
outer circumstance, the more we have cause to deny
to animals the possession of anything deserving the
name of reason, ideals, or abstract thought.   The
more, in fact, do they appear to us as mechanisms
(which is a much better word than machines, since
this latter carries with it definite connotations of
metal or wood, electricity or steam).   They are mechanisms, because their mode of operation is regular;
but they differ from any other type of mechanism
known to us in that their working is—to put it in the
most non-committal way—accompanied by emotion.
It is, to be sure, a combination of emotion with reason that we attribute to a soul; but none the less, in
popular parlance at least, the emotional side is predominant, and pure reason is set over against the
emotional content which gives soul its essence.   And

this emotional content we most definitely find running through the lives of higher animals.

The objection is easily and often raised that we have no direct knowledge of emotion in an animal, no direct proof of the existence of any purely mental process in its life. But this is as easily laid as raised. We have no direct knowledge of emotion or any other conscious process in the life of any human being save our individual selves; and yet we feel no hesitation in deducing it from others' behaviour. Although it is an arguable point whether biological science may not for the moment be better served by confining the subject-matter and terms of analysis to behaviour alone, it is a very foolhardy "behaviorist" indeed who denies the *existence* of emotion and conscious process!

But the practical value of this method of thinking is, as I say, an arguable point; it is indeed clear that a great immediate advance, especially in non-human biology, has been and may still be made by translating the uncertain and often risky terms of subjective psychology into those based upon the objective description of directly observable behaviour. However, it is equally easy to maintain, and I for one maintain it, that to omit a whole category of phenomena from consideration is unscientific, and must in the long run lead to an unreal, because limited, view of things; and that, when great detail of analysis is not required, but only broad lines and general comparison, the psychological terminology, of memory, fear, anger, curiosity, affection, is the simpler and more direct tool, and should be used to supplement and make more real the cumbersome and less complete behavioristic terminology, of modification of behaviour, fright, aggression, and the rest.

It is at least abundantly clear that, if we are to believe in the principle of uniformity at all, we must ascribe emotion to animals as well as to men the similarity of behaviour is so great that to assert the absence of a whole class of phenomena in one case, its presence in the other, is to make scientific reasoning a farce.

"Pas de cerveau—que de l'âme." Those especially who have studied birds will subscribe to this. The variety of their emotions is greater, their intensity more striking, than in four-footed beasts, while their power of modifying behaviour by experience is less, the subjection to instinct more complete. Those who are interested in the details can see from experiments, such as those recorded by Mr. Eliot Howard in his *Territory in Bird Life,* how limited is a bird's power of adjustment; but I will content myself with a single example, one of nature's experiments, recorded by Mr. Chance last year by the aid of the cinematograph—the behaviour of small birds when the routine of their life is upset by the presence of a young Cuckoo in the nest.

When, after prodigious exertions, the unfledged Cuckoo has ejected its foster-brothers and sisters from their home, it sometimes happens that one of

them is caught on or close to the rim of the nest.
One such case was recorded by Mr. Chance's camera
The unfortunate fledgling scrambled about on the
branches below the nest; the parent Pipit flew back
with food; the cries and open mouth of the ejected
bird attracted attention, and it was fed; and the
mother then settled down upon the nest as if all was
in normal order.   Meanwhile, the movements of the
fledgling in the foreground grew feebler, and one
could imagine its voice quavering off, fainter and
fainter, as its vital warmth departed.   At the next
return of the parent with food the young one was
dead.

It was the utter stupidity of the mother that was
so impressive—its simple response to stimulus—of
feeding to the stimulus of the young's cry and open
mouth, of brooding to that of the nest with something warm and feathery contained in it—its neglect
of any steps whatsoever to restore the fallen nestling
to safety.   It was almost as pitiable an exhibition
of unreason as the well-attested case of the wasp attendant on a wasp-grub, who, on being kept without
food for some time, grew more and more restless, and
eventually bit off the hind end of the grub and offered
it to what was left!

Birds in general are stupid, in the sense of being
little able to meet unforeseen emergencies; but their
lives are often emotional, and their emotions are
richly and finely expressed.   I have for years been
interested in observing the courtship and the rela-

tions of the sexes in birds, and have in my head a
number of pictures of their notable and dramatic
moments.   These seem to me to illustrate so well the
emotional furnishing of birds, and to provide such a
number of windows into that strange thing we call a
bird's mind, that I shall simply set some of them
down as they come to me.

First, then, the coastal plain of Louisiana; a pond,
made and kept as a sanctuary by that public-spirited
bird-lover Mr. E. A. McIlhenny, filled with noisy
crowds of Egrets and little egret-like Herons.   These,
in great flocks, fly back across the "Mexique Bay"
in the spring months from their winter quarters in
South America.   Arrived in Louisiana, they feed
and roost in flocks for a time, but gradually split up
into pairs.   Each pair, detaching themselves from
the flocks, choose a nesting-site (by joint delibera-
tion) among the willows and maples of the breeding
pond.   And then follows a curious phenomenon   Instead of proceeding at once to biological business in
the shape of nest-building and egg-laying, they indulge in what can only be styled a honeymoon.   For
three or four days both members of the pair are always on the chosen spot, save for the necessary vis-
its which they alternately pay to the distant feeding
grounds.   When both are there, they will spend
hours at a time sitting quite still, just touching one
another.   Generally the hen sits on a lower branch,
resting her head against the cock bird's flanks; they
look for all the world like one of those inarticulate

but happy couples upon a bench in the park in spring.
Now and again, however, this passivity of sentiment
gives place to wild excitement.   Upon some unascer-
tainable cause the two birds raise their necks and
wings, and, with loud cries, intertwine their necks.
This is so remarkable a sight that the first time I witnessed it I did not fully credit it, and only after it
had happened before my eyes on three or four separate occasions was I forced to admit it as a regular
occurrence in their lives   The long necks are so
flexible that they can and do make a complete single
turn round each other—a real true-lover's-knot!
This once accomplished, each bird then—most wonderful of all—runs its beak quickly and amorously
through the just raised aigrettes of the other, again
and again, nibbling and clappering them from base
to tip   Of this I can only say that it seemed to bring
such a pitch of emotion that I could have wished to
be a Heron that I might experience it.   This over,
they would untwist their necks and subside once more
into their usual quieter sentimentality.

     This, alas! I never saw with the less common
little White Egrets, but with the Louisiana Heron
(which should, strictly speaking, be called an egret
too); but since every other action of the two species
is (in all save a few minor details) the same, I assume that the flashing white, as well as the slate and
vinous and grey birds, behave thus.

     The greeting ceremony when one bird of the pair,
after having been away at the feeding grounds, re-

joins its mate is also beautiful. Some little time before the human watcher notes the other's approach, the waiting bird rises on its branch, arches and spreads its wings, lifts its aigrettes into a fan and its head-plumes into a crown, bristles up the feathers of its neck, and emits again and again a hoarse cry The other approaches, settles in the branches near by, puts itself into a similar position, and advances towards its mate; and after a short excited space they settle down close together. This type of greeting is repeated every day until the young leave the nest; for after the eggs are laid both sexes brood, and there is a nest-relief four times in every twenty-four hours. Each time the same attitudes, the same cries, the same excitement; only now at the end of it all, one steps off the nest, the other on. One might suppose that this closed the performance. But no: the bird that has been relieved is still apparently animated by stores of unexpended emotion, it searches about for a twig, breaks it off or picks it up, and returns with it in beak to present to the other. During the presentation the greeting ceremony is again gone through; after each relief the whole business of presentation and greeting may be repeated two, or four, or up even to ten or eleven times before the free bird flies away.

When there are numerous repetitions of the ceremony, it is extremely interesting to watch the progressive extinction of excitement. During the last one or two presentations the twig-bringing bird may

scarcely raise his wings or plumes, and will often betray an absent air, turning his head in the direction
in which he is proposing to fly off.

No one who has seen a pair of Egrets thus change
places on the nest, bodies bowed forward, plumes a
cloudy fan of lace, absolute whiteness of plumage
relieved by gold of eye and lore and black of bill, and
the whole scene animated by the repeated, excited
cry, can ever forget it. But such unforgettable scenes
are not confined to other countries. Here in England you can see as good; I have seen them on the
reservoirs of Tring, and within full view of the road
by Frensham Pond—the courtship forms and dances
of the Crested Grebe.

The Crested Grebe is happily becoming more familiar to bird-lovers in England. Its brilliant white
belly, protective grey-brown back, rippleless and effortless diving, long neck, and splendid ruff and ear-
tufts of black, chestnut, and white, conspire to make
it a marked bird. In the winter the crest is small,
and even when fully grown in spring it is usually
held close down against the head, so as to be not
at all conspicuous. When it is spread, it is almost,
without exception, in the service of courtship or love-
making. Ten years ago I spent my spring holiday
watching these birds on the Tring reservoirs. I soon
found out that their courtship, like the Herons', was
mutual, not one-sidedly masculine as in Peacocks or
fowls. It consisted most commonly in a little ceremony of head-shaking. The birds of a pair come

close, face one another, raise their necks, and half-spread their ruffs.   Then, with a little barking note, they shake their heads rapidly, following this by a slow swinging of them from side to side.   This alternate shaking and swinging continues perhaps a dozen or twenty times; and the birds then lower their standards, become normal everyday creatures, and betake themselves to their fishing or resting or preening again.   This is the commonest bit of love-making; but now and then the excitement evident even in these somewhat casual ceremonies is raised to greater heights and seems to reinforce itself.   The little bouts of shaking are repeated again and again   I have seen over eighty succeed each other uninterruptedly.   And at the close the birds do not relapse into ordinary life.   Instead, they raise their ruffs still further, making them almost Elizabethan in shape. Then one bird dives; then the other: the seconds pass.   At last, after perhaps half or three-quarters of a minute (half a minute is a long time when one is thus waiting for a bird's reappearance!) one after the other they emerge.   Both hold masses of dark brownish-green weed, torn from the bottom of the pond, in their beaks, and carry their heads down and back on their shoulders, so that either can scarcely see anything of the other confronting it save the concentric colours of the raised ruff.   In this position they swim together.   It is interesting to see the eager looks of the first-emerged, and its immediate start towards the second when it too reappears.   They approach, rapidly, until the watcher wonders what will be done to avert a collision. The answer is simple: there is no averting of a collision! But the collision is executed in a remarkable way: the two birds, when close to each other, leap up from the water and meet breast to breast, almost vertical, suddenly revealing the whole flashing white under-surface. They keep themselves in this position by violent splashings of the feet, rocking a little from side to side as if dancing, and very gradually sinking down (always touching with their breasts) towards the horizontal.

Meanwhile, they exchange some of the weed they are carrying, or at least nibbling and quick movements of the head are going on. And so they settle down on to the water, shake their heads a few times more, and separate, changing back from these performers of an amazing age-old rite—age-old but ever fresh—into the feeding- and sleeping-machines of every day, but leaving a vision of strong emotion, canalized into the particular forms of this dive and dance. The whole performance impresses the watcher not only with its strength, but as being apparently of very little direct (though possibly much indirect) biological advantage, the action being self-exhausting, not stimulating to further sexual relations, and carried out, it would seem, for its own sake

Further acquaintance with the Grebe only deepened the interest and made clearer the emotional tinge underlying all the relations of the sexes. This bird, too, has its "greeting ceremony"; but since, unlike the colonial Herons and Egrets, it makes every effort to conceal its nest, this cannot take place at its most natural moment, that of nest-relief, but must be made to happen out on the open water where there are no secrets to betray.   If the sitting bird wishes to leave the nest, and the other does not return, it flies off, after covering the eggs with weed, in search of its mate, it is common in the breeding season to see a Grebe in the "search-attitude," with neck stretched up and slightly forward and ear-tufts erected, emitting a special and far-carrying call.   When this call is recognized and answered, the two birds do nothing so simple as to fly or swim to each other, but a special and obviously exciting ceremony is gone through. The bird that has been searched for and found puts itself into a very beautiful attitude, with wings half-spread and set at right angles to the body, ruff erected circularly, and head drawn back upon the shoulders, so that nothing is visible but the brilliant rosette of the spread ruff in the centre of the screen of wings, each wing showing a broad bar of brilliant white on its dusk-grey surface.   In this position it swings restlessly back and forth in small arcs, facing towards its mate.   The discoverer meanwhile has dived; but, swimming immediately below the surface of the water, its progress can be traced by the arrowy ripple it raises.   Now and again it lifts its head and neck above the water, periscope-wise, to assure itself of its direction, and resumes its subaqueous course.   Nor does it rise just in front of the other bird, but swims

under and just beyond, and, as its mate swings round
to the new orientation, emerges in a really extraordinary attitude.   At the last it must have dived a
little deeper, for now it appears perpendicularly from
the water, with a slowish motion, slightly spiral, the
beak and head pressed down along the front of the
neck.   I compared it in my notes of ten years ago
with "the ghost of a Penguin," and that comparison
is still the best I can think of to give some idea of
the strange unreality of its appearance.   It then
settles down upon the water and the pair indulge
in one of their never-failing bouts of head-shaking.

Two mated birds rejoin each other after a few
hours' separation.   Simple enough in itself—but
what elaboration of detail, what piling on of little
excitements, what purveying of thrills!

Other emotions too can be well studied in this bird,
notably jealousy.   Several times I have seen little
scenes like the following enacted   A pair is floating
idly side by side, necks drawn right down so that the
head rests on the centre of the back.   One—generally, I must admit, it has been the cock, but I think
the hen may do so too on occasion—rouses himself
from the pleasant lethargy, swims up to his mate,
places himself in front of her, and gives a definite,
if repressed, shake of the head   It is an obvious sign
of his desire to "have a bit of fun"—to go through
with one of those bouts of display and head-shaking
in which pleasurable emotion clearly reaches its highest level in the birds' lives, as any one who has

watched their habits with any thoroughness would agree. It also acts, by a simple extension of function, as an informative symbol. The other bird knows what is meant; it raises its head from beneath its wing, gives a sleepy, barely discernible shake—and replaces the head. In so doing it puts back the possibility of the ceremony and the thrill into its slumbers; for it takes two to make love, for Grebe as for human. The cock swims off; but he has a restless air, and in a minute or so is back again, and the same series of events is run through This may be repeated three or four times.

If now another hen bird, unaccompanied by a mate, reveals herself to the eye of the restless and disappointed cock, he will make for her and try the same insinuating informative head-shake on her; and, in the cases that I have seen, she has responded, and a bout of shaking has begun. Flirtation—illicit love, if you will; for the Grebe, during each breeding season at least, is strictly monogamous, and the whole economics of its family life, if I may use the expression, are based on the co-operation of male and female in incubation and the feeding and care of the young. On the other hand, how natural and how human! and how harmless—for there is no evidence that the pretty thrills of the head-shaking display ever lead on to anything more serious.

But now observe. Every time that I have seen such a flirtation start, it has always been interrupted. The mate, so sleepy before, yet must have had one

eye open all the time. She is at once aroused to
action: she dives, and attacks the strange hen after
the fashion of Grebes, from below, with an underwater thrust of the sharp beak in the belly. Whether
the thrust ever goes home I do not know. Generally,
I think, the offending bird becomes aware of the danger just in time, and, squawking, hastily flaps off.
The rightful mate emerges. What does she do now?
Peck the erring husband? Leave him in chilly dis-
grace? Not a bit of it! She approaches with an
eager note, and in a moment the two are hard at it,
shaking their heads; and, indeed, on such occasions
you may see more vigour and excitement thrown into
the ceremony than at any other time.

Again we exclaim, how human! And again we
see to what a pitch of complexity the bird's emotional
life is tuned.

It will have been observed that in the Grebe, whose
chief skill lies in its wonderful powers of diving, these
powers have been utilized as the raw material of
several of the courtship ceremonies. This pressing
of the everyday faculties of the bird into the service
of emotion, the elevation and conversion of its useful powers of diving and underwater swimming into
ceremonials of passion, is from an evolutionary point
of view natural enough, and has its counterparts elsewhere. So in the Divers, not too distant relatives of
the Grebes, swimming and diving have their rôle in
courtship. Here too the thrilling, vertical emergence
close to the mate takes place; and there is a strange

ceremony in which two or three birds plough their way through the water with body set obliquely—hinder parts submerged, breast raised, and neck stretched forward and head downward with that strange look of rigidity or tension often seen in the courtship actions of birds.

Or, again, I once saw (strangely enough from the windows of the Headmaster's house at Radley!) the aerial powers of the Kestrel converted to the uses of courtship The hen bird was sitting in a large bush beyond the lawn. A strong wind was blowing, and the cock again and again beat his way up against it, to turn when nearly at the house and bear down upon the bush in an extremity of speed Just when it seemed inevitable that he would knock his mate off her perch and dash himself and her into the branches, he changed the angle of his wings to shoot vertically up the face of the bush; then turned and repeated the play. Sometimes he came so near to her that she would start back, flapping her wings, as if really fearing a collision. The wind was so strong—and blowing away from me—that I could not hear what cries may have accompanied the display.

A friend of mine who knows the Welsh mountains and is a watcher of birds as well, tells me that he has there seen the Peregrine Falcons do the same thing: the same thing—except that the speed was perhaps twice as great, and the background a savage rock precipice instead of a Berkshire garden.

Not only the activities of everyday life, but also

those of nest-building, are taken and used to build up the ceremonies of courtship; but whereas in the former case the actions are simply those which are most natural to and best performed by the bird, in the latter there is, no doubt, actual association between the cerebral centres concerned with nest-building and with sexual emotion in general. Thus we almost invariably find the seizing of nest-material in the beak as a part of courtship, and this is often extended to a presentation of the material to the mate. This we see in the Grebes, with the dank weeds of which their sodden nest is built; the Divers use moss in the construction of theirs, and the mated birds repair to moss banks, where they nervously pluck the moss, only to drop it again or throw it over their shoulder. Among the Warblers, the males pluck or pick up a leaf or twig, and with this in their beak hop and display before the hens; and the Peewit plucks frenziedly at grass and straws. The Adelie Penguins, so well described by Dr. Levick, make their nests of stones, and use stones in their courtship.

A curious, unnatural transference of object may sometimes be seen in these Penguins. The normal course of things is for this brave but comic creature, having picked up a stone in its beak, to come up before another of opposite sex, and, with stiff bow and absurdly outstretched flippers, to deposit it at the other's feet. When, however, there are men near the rookery, the birds will sometimes in all solemnity come up to them with their stone offering and lay it at the feet of the embarrassed or amused human being

The Adelies do not nest by their natural element the sea, but some way away from it on stony slopes and rock patches; thus they cannot employ their brilliant dives and feats of swimming in courtship, but content themselves, apart from this presentation of household material, with what Dr. Levick describes as "going into ecstasy"—spreading their flippers sideways, raising their head quite straight upwards, and emitting a low humming sound. This a bird may do when alone, or the two birds of a pair may make a duet of it. In any case, the term applied to it by its observer well indicates the state of emotion which it suggests and no doubt expresses.

The depositing of courtship offerings before men by the Penguins shows us that there must be a certain freedom of mental connection in birds. Here an act, properly belonging to courtship, is performed as the outlet, as it were, of another and unusual emotion. The same is seen in many song-birds, who, like the Sedge Warbler, sing loudly for anger when disturbed near their nest; or in the Divers, who, when an enemy is close to the nest, express the violence of their emotion by short sharp dives which flip a fountain of spray into the air—a type of dive also used as a sign of general excitement in courtship.

Or, again, the actions may be performed for their own sake, as we may say: because their performance, when the bird is full of energy and outer conditions are favourable, gives pleasure. The best-known example is the song of song-birds. This, as Eliot Howard has abundantly shown, is in its origin and essential function a symbol of possession, of a nesting territory occupied by a male—to other males a notice that "trespassers will be prosecuted," to females an invitation to settle, pair, and nest. But in all song-birds, practically without exception, the song is by no means confined to the short period during which it actually performs these functions, but is continued until the young are hatched, often to be taken up again when they have flown, or after the moult, or even, as in the Song Thrush, on almost any sunny or warm day the year round.

And finally this leads on to what is perhaps the most interesting category of birds' actions—those which are not merely sometimes performed for their own sake, although they possess other and utilitarian function, but actually have no other origin or *raison d'être* than to be performed for their own sake. They represent, in fact, true play or sport among ourselves; and seem better developed among birds than among mammals, or at least than among mammals below the monkey. True that the cat plays with the mouse, and many young mammals, like kittens, lambs, and kids, are full of play; but the playing with the mouse is more like the singing of birds outside the mating season, a transference of a normal activity to the plane of play; and the play of young animals, as

Groos successfully exerted himself to show, is of undoubted use. To be sure, the impulse to play must be *felt* by the young creature as an exuberance of emotion and spirits demanding expression; but a similar impulse must be felt for all instinctive actions. Psychologically and individually, if you like, the action is performed for its own sake; but from the standpoint of evolution and of the race it has been originated, or at least perfected, as a practice ground for immature limbs and a training and keeping ready of faculties that in the future will be needed in earnest.

We shall best see the difference between mammals' and birds' behaviour by giving some examples. A very strange one I saw in a pond near the Egret rookery in Louisiana. Here, among other interesting birds, were the Darters or Water Turkeys, curious-looking relatives of the Cormorants, with long, thin, flexible neck, tiny head, and sharp beak, who often swim with all the body submerged, showing nothing but the snake-like neck above water. One of these was sitting on a branch of swamp-cedar, solitary and apparently tranquil. But this tranquillity must have been the cloak of boredom. For suddenly the bird, looking restlessly about her (it was a hen), began to pluck at the little green twigs near by. She pulled one off in her beak, and then, tossing her head up, threw it into the air, and with dexterous twist caught it again in her beak as it descended. After five or six successful catches she missed the

twig. A comic sideways and downward glance at
the twig, falling and fallen, in meditative immobility;
and then another twig was broken off, and the same
game repeated. She was very clever at catching; the
only bird that I have seen come up to her was a
Toucan in the Zoo which could catch grapes thrown
at apparently any speed. But then the Toucan had
been specially trained—and had the advantage of a
huge capacity of bill!

Here again it might, of course, be said that the
catching of twigs is a practice for beak and eye, and
helps keep the bird in training for the serious business of catching fish. This is no doubt true; but, as
regards the evolution of the habit, I incline strongly
to the belief that it must be quite secondary—that
the bird, desirous of occupying its restless self in a
satisfying way, fell back upon a modification of its
everyday activities, just as these are drawn upon in
other birds to provide much of the raw material of
courtship. There is no evidence that young Darters
play at catching twigs as preparation for their fishing, and until there is evidence of this it is simpler
to think that the play habit here, instead of being
rooted by the utilitarian dictates of natural selection
in the behaviour of the species, as with kids or kittens, is a secondary outcome of leisure and restless-
ness combining to operate with natural aptitude—
in other words, true sport, of however simple a kind.

The commonest form of play in birds is flying play.
Any one who has kept his eyes open at the seaside

will have seen the Herring Gulls congregate in soaring intersecting spirals where the cliff sends the wind upwards. But such flights are nothing compared with those of other birds. Even the staid black-coated Raven may sometimes be seen to go through a curious performance. One I remember, all alone, flying along the side of a mountain near Oban; but instead of progressing in the conventional way, he flew diagonally upwards for a short distance, then giving a special croak with something of gusto in it, turned almost completely over on to his back, and descended a corresponding diagonal in this position. Then with a strong flap of the wings he righted himself, and so continued until he disappeared round the shoulder of the hill half a mile on. It reminded me of a child who has learnt some new little trick of step or dance-rhythm, and tries it out happily all the way home along the road. Mr. Harold Massingham has seen the Ravens' games too, and set them down more vividly than I can.[1] He also is clear that they play for the love of playing, and even believes that their love of sport has helped their downfall to rarity by rendering them too easy targets for the gunner.

Or again, at the Egret rookery in Louisiana, at evening when the birds returned in great numbers, they came back with steady wing-beats along an aerial stratum about two hundred feet up. Arrived over their nesting pond, they simply let themselves drop. Their plumes flew up behind like a comet's

[1] Massingham, '23.

tail; they screamed aloud with excitement, and, not far above the level of the trees, spread the wings so that they caught the air again, and as result skidded and side-slipped in the wildest and most exciting-looking curves before recovering themselves with a brief upward glide and settling carefully on the branches. This certainly had no significance for courtship; and I never saw it done save over the pond at the birds' return. It seemed to be simply an entertaining bit of sport grafted on to the dull necessity of descending a couple of hundred feet.

Examples could be multiplied· Rooks and Crows, our solemn English Heron, Curlew, Swifts, Snipe—these and many others have their own peculiar flying sports. What is clear to the watcher is the emotional basis of these sports—a joy in controlled performance, and excitement in rapidity of motion, in all essentials like the pleasure to us of a well-hit ball at golf, or the thrill of a rapid descent on sledge skis.

For any one to whom the evolution theory is one of the master-keys to animate nature, there must be an unusual interest in tracing out the development of lines of life that, like the birds', have diverged comparatively early from the line which eventually and through many vicissitudes led to Man.

In the birds as in the mammals, and quite separately in the two groups, we see the evolution not only of certain structural characters such as division of heart, compactness of skeleton, increase of brain-size, not only of physiological characters like warm-bloodedness or efficiency of circulation, but also of various psychical characters. The power of profiting by experience becomes greater, as does that of distinguishing between objects; and there is most markedly an increase in the intensity of emotion. It has somehow been of advantage, direct or indirect, to birds to acquire a greater capacity for affection, for jealousy, for joy, for fear, for curiosity. In birds the advance on the intellectual side has been less, on the emotional side greater: so that we can study in them a part of the single stream of life where emotion, untrammelled by much reason, has the upper hand.

BIBLIOGRAPHY

Chance, E , '22. "The Cuckoo's Secret." London, 1922.
Darwin, C , '71. "The Descent of Man, and Selection in Relation to Sex. London, 1871.
Groos, K , '98. "The Play of Animals." New York, 1898
Howard, E , '20 "Territory in Bird Life." London, 1920.
Hudson, W. H., '12. "The Naturalist in La Plata" (5th Ed.). London, 1912
Huxley, J. S., '14 and '23. (Courtship in Birds) Proc. Zool. Soc., 1914, and Proc. Linn. Soc., 1923.
Kirkman, F. B (ed), '10. "British Bird Book " London, 1910
Levick, G. M., '14 "Antarctic Penguins " London, 1914.
Massingham, H J., '23 "The Ravens." *Nation and Athenæum.* London, 21st April, 1923.
Selous, E., '01. "Bird Watching " London, 1901.
Selous, E., '05. "Bird Life Glimpses." London, 1905.

IV

SEX BIOLOGY AND SEX PSYCHOLOGY

SEX: THREE WAYS

That body has for soul an air-balloon
  Which drifts with every spiritual blast,
  Doomed, swollen thing! to leak or burst at last
Though overmuch aspiring toward the moon.

This other soul, below the animal,
  Bloating and coating body's baser parts
  With the manure of its desires and arts,
Helps flesh to grow still more corporeal.

I pray that I may still inhabit earth,
  Where grass invites the foot, and roses smell;
  Yet shall I lead my body on to dwell
In the eternal land of second birth,
If, nought contemned, each part of being's whole
Is taken up in my transmuting soul.

SEX BIOLOGY AND SEX PSYCHOLOGY [1]

"And now I see with eye serene
The very pulse of the machine."
—W WORDSWORTH.

"There is reason to believe that the processes which underlie all great work in art, literature, or science take place unconsciously, or at least unwittingly It is an interesting question to ask whence comes the energy of which this work is the expression There are two chief possibilities one, that it is derived from the instinctive tendencies which, through the action of controlling forces, fail to find their natural outlet; the other, that the energy so arising is increased in amount through the conflict between controlled and controlling forces "—W. H. RIVERS

THE biology of sex is a vast subject. Not only are there questions of sex-determination, but the whole sexual selection problem has to be considered, together with the evolutionary function of sex, and its first origin. I can only attempt, in the short space at my disposal, to deal with one or two of the chief points, and only in so far as they bear on questions of human sex psychology.

In the first place, then, we have to consider the evolutionary history of sex Of its origin we can say only that it is veiled in complete obscurity. Once

[1] Read before the British Society for Sex Psychology, October 1922.

present, however, it appears to have a definite function by making possible, through sexual reproduction, all the various combinations of any heritable variations that may arise in different individuals of a species, and so conferring greater evolutionary plasticity on the species as a whole.[2]

Primarily, sex implies only the fusion of nuclei from two separate individuals; there is no need for sex differences to exist at all. Sex differences, however, are almost universal in sexually-reproducing organisms, and represent a division of labour between the active male cell and the passive female cell, the former taking over the task of uniting the two, the latter storing up nutriment for the new individual that will result from that union.

The subsequent history of sex is, roughly speaking, the history of its invasion of more and more of the organization of its possessors. First the male as a whole, and not merely its reproductive cells, tends to become organized for finding the female. The female's whole type of metabolism is altered to produce the most efficient storage of reserve material in her ova, and later she almost invariably protects and nourishes the young during the first part of their development, either within or without her own body. Appropriate instincts are of course developed in both male and female.

At the outset there is enormous waste incurred in the liberation of sperms and ova into the water, there

[2] See East and Jones, '19.

to unite as best they may. Congress of the sexes eliminates the major part of this waste, and is universal above a certain level. This is in itself the basis for other changes. As the mind, or shall we say the psycho-neural organization, becomes more complex, the sexual instinct becomes more interwoven with the general emotional state; and a large number of animals appear not to mate unless their emotional state has been raised to a certain level. The result of this is that special actions, associated generally with bright colours or striking structures, with song or with scent, come into being.

The exact mechanism of the appearance of these courtship-displays is a much-vexed point; but it is undoubted that they only occur in animals with congress of the sexes and with minds above a certain level of complexity, and that they are employed in ceremonies between the two sexes at mating-time. There can subsist no reasonable doubt that there exists some causal connection between the associated facts.

An important point, which has been commonly overlooked, is that such characters and actions may be either developed in one sex only, or in both. In a large number of birds, such as egrets, grebes, cranes, and many others, the courtship-displays are mutual, and the characters used in them developed to a similar extent in both sexes. Such characters are therefore often not secondary sexual differences, and we had best use Poulton's term *epigamic* for them, whether they are developed in one or in both sexes.[3]

The human species, in accordance with its complexity and flexibility of brain, has epigamic characters of both kinds. Some, like voice and moustache, are different in the two sexes, others, such as colour of eyes and lips, the hairlessness of the body and grace of limbs and carriage, are common to both.

In the vertebrate stock, two main lines of evolution as regards sexual relationships may be traced. The first is predominant in mammals: here, in most species, the female will not receive the male except at fixed times, which are determined by a purely physiological mechanism, the internal secretion of the gonad (reproductive organ). Here we consequently find that the rule is for the males to fight for the possession of the females, not to display before them. In the monkeys, persumably as a result of a lessened dependence of mental upon physiological processes, bright colours and special adornments of various parts of the body are frequently developed.[4]

In the birds, on the other hand, although here too the internal secretion of the gonad delimits a period in which alone congress of the sexes can occur, it does not act for such a sharply-limited time as in the mammal, nor is it so intense as completely to override other components of the mind. As a result, general emotional stimulus may play an important part in inducing readiness to pair, and we accordingly

[3] See Huxley, '23.
[4] See Howard, '20; Carr-Saunders, '22.

find display of some sort, either by the male alone or by both sexes, present in the great majority of species.   It is at least partly in correlation with this that beauty of voice and brilliant appearance is far commoner in birds than in mammals

The monkeys represent in some way a transitional stage towards that seen in man, in whom the conditions have come to resemble those found in birds, with consequent great development of epigamic characters and actions of one sort and another, both physical and mental   Thus we see that sex, after invading and altering the conformation of the body, finally invades and alters the conformation of the mind.

As regards the other great biological question, of the determination of sex, a very few words will suffice.   In the first place I have no time to consider plants or lower animals.   In almost all higher animals that have been investigated, however, there has been found some hereditary mechanism for ensuring a rough constancy of sex-ratio.   This mechanism resides in the so-called *chromosomes* of the nucleus. These exist for the most part in similar pairs in both sexes: but one pair is dissimilar in one sex.   In mammals and man this sex is the male   Man possesses one chromosome less than woman.   He possesses only one member of this pair of special sex-chromosomes, whereas she possesses two.   All her ova are alike in possessing one, whereas half his sperms possess one, half possess none.   Therefore, when the former kind of sperms fertilize an ovum, two sex-chromosomes are present in the fertilized egg and a female results; when the latter, only one, and the offspring is male.[5]

Putting the matter in the broadest terms, we can say that there is a different balance of hereditary factors in male and female, and that this difference of balance dates from the moment of fertilization, and normally determines sex.

Various agencies may alter the balance. The chromosomes themselves may vary in what we must vaguely call their potency, or external agencies may affect it. As a result, we sometimes obtain strange abnormal individuals, in which the balance has been upset; in them development results sometimes in organisms permanently intermediate between male and female, sometimes in a change of sex at some period of development.

In insects the chromosomes appear to be predominant throughout life. In vertebrates, however, they seem to play their chief rôle in early development, ending by building up either a male or a female gonad in the early embryo. This, once produced, takes over what remains of the task of sex-determination. It secretes a specific internal secretion which in a male acts so as to encourage the growth of male organs and instincts, to suppress those of females; and vice versa in a female.

As a result of this difference we find that castration in insects, even followed by engrafting of a gonad of opposite sex, produces no effect upon other sexual

[5] See Goldschmidt, '23; Morgan, '19; Doncaster, '14.

characters; whereas it exerts a profound effect upon mammals or birds.

As a second result, we find that in vertebrates the gonads form part of what has been called the chemical directorate of the body—the interlocking system of endocrine glands, each of which is exerting an effect upon the rest The importance of this is seen in the experiments of Steinach, Sand, Voronoff, and others, who have been able to obtain a rejuvenating effect in senile mammals by increasing, by various methods, the amount of secreting reproductive organ in the body.[6]

To what then has our rapid survey led us? The actual origin of sex is lost to us in the mists of a time inconceivably remote. Its preservation once in existence, and its present all-but-universal distribution seem to be definitely associated with the biological advantage of the plasticity which it confers. Later, the primary difference between male and female—their power of producing different sorts of reproductive cells—leads on to secondary differences. These differences may be biologically speaking nonsignificant, mere accidents of the primary difference. Or they may be in the nature of a division of labour between the sexes, this division of labour usually concerning the protection of the embryo or the care of the young, or more rarely the preservation of the individual itself. Or, finally, they may concern the more efficient union of the gametes; such differences

[6] See Steinach, '20; summary in Lipschütz, '19; Voronoff, '23

may merely affect the ducts and apertures of the reproductive system, and be more or less mechanical; or they may concern the use of these systems, in the form of still mechanical instincts, or they may be concerned in some way or other with the emotional side of the animals, and consist in characters and actions which stimulate the emotions of the other sex, characters which we have termed epigamic.

It is only in higher groups that these emotion-stimulating sexual characters arise, for only in them has mind reached a sufficient degree of perfection. But even though detailed study reveals in a bird or a mammal a mental life of a complexity far more considerable than the average man would imagine, yet on the whole it is straightforward and its currents run fairly direct from stimulus to fulfilment.

When we reach man, however, the whole aspect of the matter changes.   The change is most marked, naturally, in his mental organization.   Through his powers of rapid and unlimited association, any one part of his experience can be combined with any other; through his powers of generalizing and of giving names to things, his experience is far more highly organized than that of any animal; through speech and writing he is inheritor of a continuous tradition which enormously enlarges his range of experience. Again, he can frame a purpose and thus put the objective of his actions far further into the future than can lower organisms.

There are, however, also changes of considerable

biological importance on the physical side. Man brings with him from his animal ancestors the endocrine secretory mechanism of the reproductive organs: but his life is not subordinated to it in such an iron-bound way. To start with he has gradually lost all semblance of a breeding-season. Traces of it survive in some primitive races, but in civilized communities all one can say is that the number of births may show a slight seasonal variation, and the reproductive organs are capable of function in all twelve months of the year—a state of affairs known, I believe, in no other vertebrate, or at least in no wild species.[7]

In the second place, there has been in the female a further emancipation of the sexual life. In all other mammals the female will only receive the male at certain well-defined periods, which in their turn depend on cyclical changes in the ovaries. In man this restriction has been overcome, and, in spite of the survival of a certain degree of cyclical change in feeling, neither sex is restricted any longer to certain physically-determined periods for the consummation of its sexual life. This is, we may say, a triumph of mind over matter in the human organism, of the mental elements of the sexual life over the purely physical elements.

This is not to deny that the sexual life of man is dependent upon the reproductive hormones. It is apparently necessary for proper activation of the

[7] See Carr-Saunders, '22, ch. v, and M. Stopes.

sexual centres in the brain that there should occur a continuous liberation of secretion from the reproductive organs into the blood. Again, the mental activities of man are so much more important than those of other forms that even the cessation of activity of the reproductive organs, for instance in the female at the change of life, or even their total removal, need not prevent the continuation, albeit in a modified form, of the sexual life in its varied indirect manifestations.

Before attempting to probe the intricacies of the mental side of the subject, we had better see what we can learn of the physical. Let us first remind ourselves of one or two facts gained from animal experimentation. In the first place, in mammals the activation of the sexual instincts of one or the other sex appears to be completely or almost completely under the control of the internal secretions of the reproductive organs. Steinach and others have taken new-born male guinea-pigs and have removed their testes and grafted ovaries in their place. The result has been an animal almost completely feminized both as regards body and mind. In some of the animals milk was secreted, and when this occurred they would act as foster-mothers to new-born guinea-pigs of other parents. The reverse operation, the masculinization of females, was equally successful, the animals growing large and showing all the instincts of a normal male and none of those of a normal female.

A similar dependence of behaviour on gonad is

seen in fowls Here nature makes a number of experiments, which have recently been studied by Dr. Crew of Edinburgh When the ovaries of a hen are affected by a certain type of tumour, the bird stops laying, her comb and wattles enlarge to the size of a cock's, her spurs grow, she begins to crow, her plumage changes at the moult and becomes cock-like, and finally she becomes indistinguishable from a male. Indistinguishable, even in behaviour: her years of feminine routine in laying and brooding are forgotten: the secretion of the altered ovary now apparently resembles that of a testis and stimulates centres of the brain which would otherwise have remained permanently dormant. She struts and crows, fights and mates, and the memory of the previous part of her life is for all practical purposes lost, since the centres for female activity are no longer stimulated at all.

Various workers have even experimentally produced a state of hermaphroditism in mammals by simultaneous grafting of portions of testes and ovary: the behaviour here oscillates between male and female.[8]

It is quite clear from these and other facts that in higher vertebrates there are present in every individual of either sex the nervous connections which give the possibility of either male or female behaviour; but that normally only one of these two possibilities is realized, since for the potentiality of action given by the nervous connections to become

[8] See Lipschütz, '19; Goldschmidt, '23.

actual as behaviour it is necessary for the nervous system to be activated by the secretion of one or other of the reproductive organs.   Castrated animals fail to realize either possibility of normal sex-behaviour, although their nervous machinery is untouched.

There are, further, some facts of observation which, even if they have not yet been fully analysed by experiment, still throw light on the matter.   Although many of the most familiar birds—fowls, pheasant, peacock, duck, finches, and so forth—have bright-coloured males and drab females, with marked difference of behaviour between the sexes, there are, as we have seen, many others, such as herons, divers, swans, grebes, moorhens, and auks, in which the sexes are alike in plumage and furthermore show what may be called a "mutual" courtship in which both male and female play similar rôles.   In this latter class it seems clear that the secretions of the male and female reproductive organs must be more alike than in the markedly dimorphic species: and this is borne out by some strange facts regarding not merely the courtship but the actions concerned with pairing itself.   In the crested grebe and the little grebe, for example, close observation has shown that either member of the pair may assume the passive "female" attitude or the active "male" attitude in pairing: and in the moorhen we meet with the still more extraordinary phenomenon of double pairing, in which an act of pairing with male and female in normal position is immediately followed by a second act in which the normal position is reversed.[9] it would appear in such cases that the similarity of male and female internal secretion is so great that quite slight changes in nervous or metabolic activity can cause the nervous centres for the opposite sex's mode of behaviour to become activated.

In human beings we are confronted with various grades of sexual organization and behaviour besides the typically feminine and the typically masculine. In the first place it is matter of common knowledge that many women, who so far as their physical reproductive capacity goes are perfectly normal, show various mental traits which are more characteristic of men, and vice versa. What is more, the "masculinoid" woman (to use the current jargon) tends physically also to be less feminine, to have the feminine secondary sexual characteristics in stature, form of skeleton, distribution of fat, breasts, etc.— less strongly developed than normal, while the "feminoid" man shows the reverse tendency.[10]

In trying to analyse these facts further, we are brought up against new depths of complication It is becoming ever clearer that the gonads do not operate as independent organs, but in conjunction with the whole of the rest of the endocrine system— thyroid, pituitary, adrenal, and the rest. In the first place, it seems to be established that the reproduc-

[9] See Selous, '02, Huxley, 14
[10] See Blair Bell, '16.

tive organs must be in some way activated by other ductless glands before they become normal, just as they in their turn must activate the sexual centres in the brain. This phase of the matter is being investigated by many workers to-day; provisionally we may say that pituitary and adrenal cortex are especially concerned. In the second place the gonads, once activated and in normal working order, react upon the other ductless glands. It thus comes about that the relative proportion or relative activity of the parts of the whole ductless gland system is different in male and female. Blair Bell is the protagonist of this view. A woman is a woman, he says, not merely because of her ovaries, but because of all her internal secretions, of her endocrine balance as a whole.

It cannot be said that we have any certainty on the details of this subject. It is clear, however, that some such fundamental difference does exist, and it is therefore further probable that if a woman has a thyroid, say, or an adrenal which for some reason (and there are many possible reasons) is producing an amount of secretion abnormal for a woman but more like that which is produced by a man, she will, in spite of her ovaries, be more masculine in tendency.

I will content myself with one example. The cortex of the adrenal gland, if active beyond a certain measure, assists the development of male, prevents the development of female, characters. Women with adrenal tumours frequently develop moustache and beard and other appanages of the male. One presumes that a slight preponderance of the adrenal cortex in the normal endocrine make-up will lead to a less feminine type of woman than normal. I repeat that we are but on the verge of the matter and that premature speculation is certainly risky and probably fallacious. But all the same, there is very little doubt that we are on the right track, and that we shall have to search for the finer shades of temperamental difference between man and woman not so much in differences in the quality of the secretion of testis or ovary as in differences of balance in what the Americans call the "endocrine make-up." [11]

There is, however, also the possibility of difference in the quality of gonad secretion, and of recent years Steinach and his followers have been claiming that this may be at the bottom of many cases of so-called "perversion of sexual instinct." The latest claim of this school is that homosexual men may be rendered heterosexual in instinct by removal of their testes and implantation of a testis from a sexually normal person—from a man, for example, who is being operated on for cryptorchidism. It is frankly impossible as yet to say whether their conclusions are well founded: a very much larger series of cases will be necessary, and the possibility of suggestion's action must be eliminated. It is well to remember, however, that there is no theoretical objection to the

[11] See Vincent, '21; Harrow, '23.

possibility. We know that in various lower animals, such as moths and flies, the balance between the male- and female-determining factors in the chromosomes may be altered in certain crosses, and that this altered balance in the constitution is reflected in some cases in a state permanently intermediate between male and female, in others by a reversal of sex at some point during development. For various reasons we should not usually expect reversal in mammals; but if such abnormal balance should exist in the constitution, as it well might, we should expect a gonad secreting an abnormal, intermediate secretion. This we might also expect as the result of certain accidents of embryonic life, as actually happens in the abnormal female cattle known to farmers as free-martins. These animals are always born co-twin to a male, and their abnormality is due to the blood-systems of the embryonic membranes of the twins having fused, so that the secretion of the developing male's gonad acts upon the developing female.

Further light on abnormally-directed sex-instinct is thrown by recent analysis of abnormal domestic animals by Crew.[12] In both goats and swine he finds that by far the commonest form of sexual abnormality is one in which the external appearance, at least in youth, is so nearly female as to raise no question in the mind of the casual observer; about the time of maturity, however, male secondary sex

[12] Crew, '23.

characters begin to develop, including male instincts; and dissection reveals the presence of a double set of ducts—the female uterus and vagina, the male epididymis and vas deferens, but only a single uniform reproductive organ, and that always a testis. The simplest explanation (although it is admittedly tentative) appears to be that the testis has not been activated during embryonic and juvenile life, and that therefore until puberty the animal, though really male, has been physiologically in a neutral state, which permits the growth of the internal apparatus proper to both sexes. Externally, the "neutral" condition approximates more closely to the female type, and the animal is thus first classed as a female. Some other gland is then responsible for the second activation at puberty, and this occurs in a normal manner.

This is of considerable interest, since it appears that in man too the largest class of sexually abnormal individuals are those whose external appearance is almost or quite feminine, but who possess male instincts. It is at least probable that examination will show that they, too, or many of them, will be of the type described above—males with delayed activation of testis, a consequent classification as female at birth, and a girl's upbringing, with male instincts arising in the unhappy creature at puberty.

It is the fashion nowadays to write down abnormal sexual psychology wholly to the account of the mind, to an abnormal development with causes entirely psychological. It is clear, however, that if some abnormal individuals can be cured by implantation, and others are abnormal owing to an early failure of activation, this conception falls to the ground, and the Freudian is robbed of some of his most cherished examples. .

In any case, the work on animals definitely shows that, unless the mechanism of activation of instinct by gonad secretion has altered between animal and man more than we have any right to postulate a priori, the quality of gonad secretion and the balance of all the endocrines has to be taken into account far more than is done by the average psycho-analyst

This, however, is not to say that the genesis of our attitude towards sex, our sexual behaviour, and our general mental organization in so far as modified by sex, is not normally determined for the most part by purely psychological causes. If there is a physical abnormality, this will react upon the mental, but in the vast majority of cases the physical variation will not take the individual beyond the limits of normality, and when the normal physical limits are not exceeded, the wide range of mental variation still observable is to be ascribed to psychological causes. In other words, abnormal sexual behaviour and instinct may be due either to physiological or psychological abnormality, and the latter is probably the commoner cause.

I am not competent to attempt to treat of the vast and complex psychological aspect of the sex-problem which the analytical psychologists have opened up to such an extent within the last few years; I can only deal with it in the broadest way, and content myself rather with stating than with solving problems.

As regards the place of sex in our mental organization, there are two contradictory extremes possible. Either all ideas connected with the physical side of sex may be repressed with great vehemence, and the sexual contribution to various emotions ignored or dismissed, while a constant attempt is made at sublimation; or else there is little or no repression beyond that necessitated by convention and custom, sexual matters are taken at their physical face value, and sublimation is not consciously attempted and exists only to a negligible amount.

There is no doubt that the first alternative represents one of the commonest neuroses of modern life, and one in which an interpretation on principles made familiar by psycho-analysis is the most satisfactory. Repression, through whatever cause initiated (and psychologists, I understand, are coming more and more to recognize that chronic misuse of the mind as well as single violent shocks may be effective), leads to a more or less complete dissociation of two parts of the mind, of which one only is in the main connected with the conscious personal life. As a result, curious phenomena are met with There is, it is true, a constant effort necessary to keep life a-going with the aid of an incomplete mental organization; but when satisfaction is attained, its very rarity brings with it a certain glow, an irradiation of peculiarly pleasurable nature. Furthermore, dissociation in most cases is not complete; now and again, and especially when there is successful sublimation—in some people when in love, in others with religious ecstasy, in others again with some form of art—now and again re-association of the parts occurs, and there is an extraordinary sense of the irruption of some vast beneficent force, some great extra-personal flood of soul, into the meagre stream of everyday life. The lives of a certain number of saints and ascetics, mystics and poets, abound with phenomena of this sort; and apparently the sense of value attaching to the occasional complete attainment of such satisfactory states of the soul, combined with the conscious daily quest for sublimation which is inevitable when the most important part of the primitive emotions are repressed, is such a vivid experience that it satisfies the mind and enables such persons to carry on, and to do work sometimes of the highest value.

On the other hand, men and women with this type of mental development naturally tend to be unstable; they cannot be sure of their capacity, whether for routine work or creative thought or spiritual experience, from day to day. Their mental life has a tendency to wear thin, their sense of effort and struggle to increase and lead to breakdown. It is in the long run an unsatisfactory way of organizing the psyche, because the conscious mind has less than it ought to have upon which to fall back

The opposite extreme is equally unsatisfactory. If individuals of the first type are trying to build high without adequate foundations, those of the second are mistaking the foundations for a complete building. A dissociation of a different type occurs in them—a dissociation due to lack of use, to a mere failure to connect up that part of the mind concerned with sexual emotion with a great many of the mind's other activities. Thus the sexual side has few and lower values associated with it than it might, and other possibilities of thought and feeling and action remain as mere possibilities, never realized in actuality. The result is a definitely incomplete personality of a more or less arrested or rudimentary type.

Those are the extremes of course there are all intermediates between them. They may crop up with apparent spontaneity, determined more by the hereditary constitution of the man or woman than by external happenings: or they may be mainly or at least largely determined by the accidents of the environment during the period before maturity. One of the most potent factors in the environment will be the attitude of the parents towards sexual matters. On the one hand they may adopt the common, horror-stricken attitude towards sex, hushing it up, making it clear to the sensitive mind of childhood that there is something thoroughly bad about it, and so laying the best possible foundations for future repression. Or, on the other hand, they may openly adopt the psycho-analytic view as to the rôle of sex in the development of mind, may further believe that the fullest analysis and self-knowledge is always desirable, and may accordingly be pointing out to the child interpretations of its actions and sayings in terms of sex, familiarizing it with sex from the outset, not merely not discouraging but actually encouraging reference to sexual matters. This will tend, *ceteris paribus*, to the development of a mind in which many of the more complex mental operations will not usually persist because the subject will be continually unbuilding them into their constituent parts, of which sex will be the most unvarying and important.

Both these types are to my judgment obviously unsatisfactory. The ideal organization of the mind must be one in which first there is a minimum of waste of energy, secondly a maximum realization of potentiality. The operations of mind may further be thought of from two different angles—a subserving the biological needs of the organism, or as ends in themselves. From the first point of view, thought is action *in posse*· efficiency and full utilization of energy are here the requirements, and it is obvious that any method which even partially separates one part of the mental organization from the rest must be a poor one, that a refusal to face any portion of reality, such as, in our special case, the physical side of sex, must put the organism at a disadvantage in a world in which that portion of reality plays, as it obviously does, an important rôle.

The correct type of organization is one of the type which has been developed over and over again in the course of evolution, for different functions: it is the hierarchical one, in which some parts are dominant, others subordinate, the dominant parts helpless without the subordinate, the subordinate different, through the fact of their subordination, from what they would otherwise have been, doing most of the hard work, but under the guidance of the dominant.   Only in this way is a unitary organization arrived at in which there is the minimum of waste, of antagonism between the parts.

The psycho-analysts have, by analysing the pathology of mind, shown us how waste of energy may arise in particular cases, and so make it easier for us to avoid it in general.

One may recognize the merits of Freud as an investigator without accepting all or even the majority of his conclusions.   As the late W. H. Rivers pointed out, Freud will always be remembered in the history of psychology because he introduced new ideas and new methods into the science.   Previous workers had discovered the realm of the subconscious; but they had not discovered the real nature of its relation to the rest of the mental organization.   Freud pointed out that there was often a biological value attached to the power of forgetting as well as to that

of remembering, and that in any case in most of us
a large amount of experience is rendered unconscious
by suppression, or an attempt made to force it into
the unconscious by repression. He and his followers
and other schools of psychologists have pointed out
the importance of unresolved conflicts in determining thought and behaviour, and have made it clear
that in the ordinary civilized community of to-day a
large proportion of those conflicts arise out of difficulties connected with the sex-instinct. And, even
if we reject the extreme claims made by many Freud-
ians, we must admit that psycho-analysis has shown
that many cases of actual perversion of instinct may
be cured by analytic methods, and that sex occupies
a very much larger space in the mind than was previously supposed. It had not been previously supposed, because of the fact that it tends to appear in
consciousness in disguised form—either sublimated
and thus intertwined with other emotions and instincts or with unusual objects, or else rationalized
as something else, or kept below the surface of consciousness as an unfulfilled wish; and because there
is a resistance in most of us to recognizing its importance

This revolution in our thought has proved very
unpalatable to many. In just the same way as a
large proportion of Darwin's opponents opposed him
because they believed that to accept man's simian
origin was a repulsive degradation, so many of the
opponents of psycho-analysis oppose it because they

believe that to ascribe this huge rôle to sex in the genesis of our psyche is a repulsive degradation.

To my mind there are two very general questions which the student of human sex psychology now has to face, if he takes not necessarily the whole but the central theses of psycho-analysis, however much pruned, as proven. The first is this: granted that sex does play such a large part, especially in early years, in the genesis of our mental organization, is it desirable that the average adult or adolescent should, by analysis, be given full self-knowledge on the subject?

The second is this: granted that sex does penetrate into more corners of mind in man than in lower organisms, is this really a regrettable thing, or can we find any grounds for believing it to be desirable or biologically progressive?

To answer this we shall have to go back a little to first principles, and consider, however briefly, certain facts as to the march of evolution.

Evolution is essentially progressive. It proceeds on the whole in a certain direction, and that direction is on the whole towards a realization of what seems to us to have positive value. The direction, however, as a matter of fact, is most striking when we consider the maximum level attained, much less so when we consider the average, not at all when we look at the minimum

The method or mechanism of progress may differ in different types, and it does differ in man from that which is found in other mammals. In most higher animals progress is brought about chiefly by natural selection operating upon individuals, although in a few forms selection operates chiefly upon groups of communities: in both cases the changes in the inherited constitution of the species are the important changes In man, however, in all except the very early stages of his development, changes in inherited constitution have been small and unimportant, and the chief changes of evolutionary significance have been those in tradition, selection among individuals has been of relatively little importance, and selection has fallen mainly upon groups and, to an ever-increasing extent, upon their ideas and traditions.

In spite of differences in method as between different types of organism, the tendency has been in the same direction—towards a possibility of greater control, greater independence, greater complexity, and greater regulation or harmony.

Looked at from the evolutionary point of view, the moving, dynamic point of view, we have to think of human sex-psychology in yet another way. So far we have been treating it as what it is; now we must think of what it may become.

The general rule in evolution—the natural and obvious rule—is that acquisitions are not thrown away when change occurs, but built upon, utilized for some new function. The endostyle of the lowest chordates, part of a very primitive type of feeding mechanism, was converted, when they changed their mode of life, into the thyroid gland: the parathyroids develop from the remains of the gill-apparatus when gills are discarded for lungs: the secondary sexual differences which originate as accidental consequence of the primary difference between the sexes are, over and over again, elaborated into special characters employed in courtship.

So the sex-instinct and its associated emotion, at first simply one among a number of separate and scarcely-correlated instincts, has in man become the basis for numerous new mental functions.   It can enter into the composition of various emotions, though its character is often disguised and its presence often undetected.   It contributes to some of the most exalted states of mind which we can experience. The sexual relationship, which in lower animals involves neither contact nor even propinquity, but simply simultaneous discharge of reproductive cells, and in most animals is a purely temporary affair, is very different in man.   Even in those birds and non-human mammals in which the sexes remain associated for long periods or permanently, the different departments of life are more in water-tight compartments, the psychical activity is subordinate to the physiological: in man the physiological side, though of course still basic and necessary, is more— and can be much more—subordinate to the psychological, and all parts of the mental life interpenetrate to a much greater extent; so that the sex-instinct may become transformed by a psychological process roughly analogous to the transformation of physical energy, and reappear in altered guise in various other activities of mind.

If we look at the matter broadly, we see that man is in a period of evolutionary transition as regards sex. We found previously that the greatest change connected with sex which has been made in the evolution of higher animals was the change by which there was evolved a brain and mind with associated sense-organs in which accurate perception of objects at a distance could occur, a mechanism which really dominated the working of the organism as a whole, and in which memory and emotion seemed to play an important part. Once this happened, the sex-instinct could be linked up with general emotional reactions and connected with external objects capable of inducing emotion.

What was the result? That in every group possessing such a type of mind, epigamic characters of a beautiful or striking or bizarre nature were evolved. This first linking-up of sex with mind produced, eventually, a large proportion of the beauty of the organic world. It coloured and adorned not only many a bird, but even newts and fish and spiders; it helped elicit song and music from mere sounds and noises; it moulded our own bodies, coloured our lips and eyes, and everywhere helped in adding grace to mere serviceableness; it saw to it that, as St. Paul puts it, "even our uncomely parts have an abundant comeliness." But, as we have just pointed out, its connection with the mind's higher centres was in all pre-human forms still temporary, under the control of cyclical physiological changes, and the mind as a whole was still constructed in compartments, so that different instincts and different experiences did not necessarily or even usually come in contact with each other.

The next great change is being made now; it concerns a further development of mind and a consequent fresh mode of connection of sex with mental life. As we have outlined above, this change in mind consists in the tendency towards uniting the different parts of the psyche, both those portions given by heredity and the modification due to experience, into a single organic whole, and in making this whole more dominant over the other aspects of the organism; the consequent tendency as regards the relationship of sex to the organism is towards taking it out of its single groove, its water-tight compartment, and bringing it into more complete and more permanent union with the rest of the mind. Furthermore, the main change and the consequent change as regards sex are both of a biologically progressive nature.

We are now, I think, owing to our taking this broad biological view, in a better position to make up our minds as to some at least of the difficulties which beset us to-day in any attempt to deal squarely with the relation of sex to human life. It is true that some of these difficulties are permanent. The synthesis of a unitary and comprehensive mental organization can never be an easy task. The child is endowed with a number of instinctive tendencies which, as in animals, each tend whenever aroused to occupy the whole mental field to the exclusion of all others, producing divergence and lack of co-ordination instead of unity and organization. Then again, the experience of any one individual may be highly unusual. For the child to co-ordinate his various tendencies with each other and with his own experience and with the tradition and experience of the race must always be difficult, and there will always be some failures.

There is another permanent difficulty, a biological disharmony, in the fact that sexual maturity in man comes several years before general maturity, and that again, at least in any state of civilization which we can at present imagine as practicable, several years before the economic possibility of marriage. There will always be crises of adolescence; there will always be suffering and difficulty due to this disharmony in time between the origin of the full sexual instinct and the possibility of its proper satisfaction.

However, granted these permanent difficulties, there are others which may be reduced or made to disappear. Granted that we have to organize our minds into a whole, we can see the general plan on which we should aim at organizing it. We must aim first at having no barriers between different parts of the mind.   Every attempt must be made in the education of children to prevent there being a stigma attached to one whole section of mental life, and so to avoid its partial or total dissociation from the rest.   On the other hand, the absence of barriers does not imply the absence of any relation of subordination or dominance of one part to another. One of the most important biological generalizations is that progressive evolution is accompanied by the rise of one part to dominance and, whenever there are many parts to be considered, by the arrangement of the rest in some form of hierarchy, each part being subordinate to one above, dominant to one below.   It is such a hierarchy which we must try to construct in our mental organization.

It is obviously impossible here to go into the whole question of values and ideals, but it is clear to any one who has given the briefest reflection to the subject that there are certain values, æsthetic, intellectual, and moral, which are ultimate for the mind of man, certain ideals—of truth and honesty, intellectual satisfaction, righteousness or at least freedom from the sense of sin or guilt, completeness and self-realization, unselfishness and serviceableness and so forth—which (though perhaps in varying proportions) are by common consent accepted as the highest: and further that the greater the attempt to deepen and broaden these, to increase their mental intensity and to widen their range and association, the more they tend to emerge into something in-

creasingly unitary, in which it is seen that honesty
is also beautiful and useful, that intellectual satisfaction is in the long run serviceable to the community, that unselfishness to be effective requires
thought and will besides mere altruistic emotion,
that one of the greatest aids to any genuine righteousness is an æsthetic love of beautiful things that prevents our doing ugly things, and so *ad infinitum*.

The proper way, then, to build the sex instinct into
the mental system is not to have its stimulation cause
a merely physiological and uninhibited desire for its
gratification, nor to bring about a forcible repression
and an attempt to break connection between it and
the other parts of the mind.

The desirable method is to have free connection
between it and the dominant ideas, so that its stimulation brings about a stimulation of them too. This
leads, as a matter of experience, to the incorporation
of the sexual emotion in the dominant ideas, or we
had better say an interpenetration of one with the
other, so that the sexual emotion is no longer simply
sexual emotion, but is become part of something very
much larger and very much better. Let the great
writers say in their few words what I should say
much worse in many.

Wordsworth's "sense sublime of something far
more deeply interfused" opens a window on to the
general process of sublimation: and Blake's description of the physical union of the sexes as "that . . .
on which the soul expands her wing" is an epitome

of a particular aspect of our particular problem.   Or again, when St. Paul says "Am I not free?" or "All things are lawful unto me," he means that by subordinating all sides of himself to his highest ideals, he has reached that state in which what he does is right to him because he only wants to do what is right.   (True that, as he himself confesses, he is not always able to keep in that state: but when he is in it, he attains that complete freedom which is the subordination of lower to higher desire)

Physiologically speaking, the activation of the sex instinct, when the connection is made in this way, arouses the higher centres, and these react upon the centres connected with the sex instinct, modifying their mode of action.   The nett result is thus that both act simultaneously to produce a single whole of a new type.   Processes of this nature are common in the nervous system, as has been shown for instance by Hughlings Jackson, Head, and Rivers.[13]

Thus the higher, dominant parts of the mind are strengthened by their connection with such lower parts as the simple sex instinct, and the sex instinct is able to play a rôle in any operation of the mind, however exalted, in which emotion is in any way concerned.   Rivers believes that the actual conflict between controlled and controlling parts of the mind is a potent generator of mental "energy"; and adds, "whatever be the source of the energy, however, we can be confident that by the process of sublimation

[13] See Rivers, '20, chs. iv, xviii.

the lives upon which it is expended take a special course, and in such case it is not easy to place any limit to its activity. We do not know how high the goal that it may reach." [14]

The change is thus on the one side from the relative independence of the sex instinct towards its subordination to a position in a hierarchy of mental process, but on the other from a rigid limitation of its scope towards a greater universality by establishing connections with all other parts of the mind. Further, there is also a change towards greater dominance and "self-determination" of the mental as against the physical.

A great many of the difficulties which beset us, both as individuals and as communities, come from the fact that both these changes are only in process of being made, and are (even approximately) complete only in a very small number of persons.

Lack of restraint is failure to construct a properly-working hierarchy. That is a very simple example. Less easy to analyse but equally vicious, are the innumerable cases in which some sort of equilibrium is only attained not by a free interaction of dominant and subordinate parts, but by repression. Conflicts arise, which persist, either in an open form or in the subterranean regions of the unconscious. In either case they tend to be projected by the subject into his ideas of other people. This projection, or interpretation of external reality in terms of one's self, is

[14] Rivers, '20, p. 158.

a curious and almost universal attribute of the human mind. The most familiar example is perhaps the anthropomorphism which in religion after religion has invested the powers of the universe with human form, human mental process, human personality—or at least with form, mind, and personality similar to those of man; while a very simple case is that in which certain neurotic types project their depression so as to colour everything that comes into their cognizance a gloomy black.

In the sphere of sex this process is, alas, most potently at work. The man in whom the sexual instinct still lives a more or less independent, uninhibited life of its own, tends—unless he has special evidence to the contrary, and often even then—to interpret the behaviour and the minds of others in the terms familiar to himself, and to suppose that they too must be stopped by the fear of punishment or of loss of caste if they are not to commit excesses.

On the other hand, those in whom there is a constant conflict with a sexual origin project it here, there, and everywhere into the breasts of those they know, and interpret others' motives in terms of their own repressed wishes.

Furthermore, most of our existing laws and customs are based on a state of society in which the changes to which we have referred had not progressed as far as they have to-day, and man's psychology was a little less removed from that of other mammals.

The result is that those who attempt the complete emancipation possible to a properly-organized mind are confronted first by the lag of our institutions and traditions, and secondly by the unconcealed suspicion of all those—and they are as yet the large majority—in which the conflicts arising out of sex are unresolved. It is from the sum of those conflicts that the spirit prevalent with regard to sex to-day derives its character—shocked and shamefaced as regards one's own sexual life, vindictive and grudging as regards the difficulties of others. The bulk of men and women cannot treat sexual problems in a scientific spirit, because of the store of bottled-up emotion in the wrong place that they have laid up for themselves by their failure to come to proper terms with their sexual instincts. The soul should grow to deserve the words Crashaw wrote of St. Theresa—"O thou undaunted daughter of desires!" But this the soul of such disharmonic beings can never do.

This brings us to our other pressing question. Should the results of psycho-analytic methods, the knowledge that the sex instinct is fundamental and is interwoven into the roots of the highest spiritual activities—should the inculcation and demonstration of this be part of education? Some would say yes, and would argue that to know oneself is essential to a proper realization of one's capacities. Personally I am extremely doubtful of the correctness of this answer. Knowledge of the processes of digestion is not necessary to digest well—so long as we go on digesting well: it is only necessary when we digest badly.   In that case the processes involved are automatic: but even in processes which require a great deal of learning, we find a similar state of affairs.   A man can become expert at, say, a game requiring the most delicate adjustments of hand and eye without analysing the processes he employs, but by practising them as finished articles, so to speak; and it is equally obvious that Shakespeare and Shelley and Blake and other great writers produced their works without the least analytical knowledge of the obscure and rather unpleasant processes which, if we are to believe the critics who psycho-analyse dead authors in the pages of Freudian journals, were "really" at work below the surface.   Analysis constitutes a serious surgical operation for the mind, and, as one of the leading Austrian psycho-analysts has recently said, we do not want to perform this operation on healthy people any more than we want to open their abdomens merely for the sake of seeing that their viscera are normal.

If matters concerning sex are treated properly during a child's development and education, the necessity for psycho-analysis and any extension of analytic knowledge of the foundations of one's own mind that it may bring is done away with.   If it can be ensured that there is no obvious avoidance of the subject leading to repression in the child's mind, and on the other hand no undue prominence given to it so that a morbid curiosity is aroused, a large proportion of the conflicts that now arise could be avoided. The other necessity is that there should be provision for sublimation—in art or music, in social service or in one's own work, in religion, or, in modified form, in sport or romance.

It is perfectly possible, in such case, for mental development to proceed naturally and comparatively smoothly towards a unified organization of the type of which we have spoken. Psycho-analysis would not help a boy or girl developing in such a way, any more than would a study of all the characters we have inherited from our simian forefathers help us to realize our specifically human possibilities. On the other hand, when the intellectual desire to know things for their own sake is aroused, as it is in most boys and girls between the ages of about fourteen and twenty, then just as it is good, in order to get a true picture of the universe, for them to know and be presented with the evidence for man's evolution from lower forms, so it is good for the same reason to give them an account of their psychological organization, including evidence for the rôle which sex plays in the genesis of higher mental activities— without, however, any necessity for psychological experiments in burrowing into their own foundations. In this case such knowledge would have the additional value of putting them on their guard against allowing themselves to be prejudiced by their own incompletely-adjusted conflicts.

We are all of us too prone to think that a phenomenon is somehow "explained," or interpreted better,
by analysing it into its component parts or discovering its origin than by studying it in and for itself.

The new type of mental organization acquired by
man permits of wholly new types of mental process,
of a complexity as far exceeding those that we deduce
in brutes as does the physical organism of a dog or
an ant that of a polyp or a protozoan: and it is part
of our business to realize those possibilities to the
fullest extent.

To sum up, then, biological investigation in the
first place shows us how certain abnormalities of sexual psychology may be more easily interpreted as
caused by comparatively simple physical abnormalities than by the more complex distortions of psychological origin dealt with by psycho-analysis.   In the
second place, by giving us a broader *aperçu* than can
otherwise be gained over the evolution of sex and the
direction visible in biological history, it clears up
to a certain extent some of the difficulties which the
discoveries of the psycho-analytic school have rendered acute.

If the changes in the relation of the sex instinct to
the rest of the mind, which I have spoken of above
as being in operation at present, should one day
progress so far as to be more or less carried through
in a majority, or in a dominant section of the population, the whole outlook of society towards the sex

problem would be changed, and the laws and institutions and customs connected with it completely remodelled.

The most pressing task of those who are thinking over the problem of sex in human life will often be the relief of suffering and the removal of abuses: but the broader view should never be forgotten, and every attempt should be made to think constructively with a view to realizing the enormous possibilities that such a change would bring about.

BIBLIOGRAPHY

Blair Bell, '16. "The Sex Complex." London, 1916.

Carr-Saunders, '22. "The Population Problem." Oxford, 1922.

Crew, '23 Proc. Roy. Soc. (B.). London, 1923.

Cunningham, J. T., '00 "Sexual Dimorphism in the Animal Kingdom." London, 1900.

Doncaster, L., '14. "The Determination of Sex." Cambridge, 1914.

East and Jones, '19. "Inbreeding and Outbreeding." Philadelphia, 1919

Ellis, Havelock, '10. "Studies in the Psychology of Sex." Philadelphia, 1910.

Freud. "The Psychology of the Unconscious."

Goldschmidt, R., '23. "The Mechanism and Physiology of Sex-Determination." London, 1923.

Harrow, B., '23. "Glands in Health and Disease." London, 1923.

Howard, E., '20. "Territory in Bird Life." London, 1920.

Huxley, '14. (Reversed Pairing, Grebe) Proc. Zool. Soc. London, 1914.

Huxley, '23. (Courtship and Display) Proc. Linnean Soc. London, 1923.

Jung, '20. "Analytical Psychology." London, 1920.

Lipschütz, '19. "Die Pubertatsdruse." Bern, 1919.

Marshall, '23. "The Physiology of Reproduction" (2nd Ed). Cambridge, 1923.

Meisenheimer, J., '21. "Geschlecht und Geschlechter." Jena, 1921.

Morgan, '19. "The Physical Basis of Heredity." Philadelphia, 1919

Rivers, '20. "Instinct and the Unconscious." Cambridge, 1920

Selous, E , '20. (Moorhen) *Zoologist* [4] 6. London, 1902.

Steinach J., '20. Verjüngung, Leipzig, 1920.

Stopes, Marie. "Married Love."

Tansley, '20. "The New Psychology." London, 1920

Vincent, Swale, '21. "Internal Secretion and the Ductless Gland" (2nd Ed.). London, 1921.

Voronoff, S., '23. "Greffes Testiculaires." Paris, 1923.

V

PHILOSOPHIC ANTS:

A BIOLOGIC FANTASY

PHILOSOPHIC——ANTS?

Amoeba has her picture in the book,
  Proud Protozoon!—Yet beware of pride.
  All she can do is fatten and divide;
She cannot even read, or sew, or cook . . .

The Worm can crawl—but has no eyes to look:
  The Jelly-fish can swim—but lacks a bride:
  The Fly's a very Ass personified:
And speech is absent even from the Rook.

The Ant herself cannot philosophize—
  While Man does that, and sees, and keeps a wife,
And flies, and talks, and is extremely wise . . .
  Will our Philosophy to later Life
Seem but a crudeness of the planet's youth,
Our Wisdom but a parasite of Truth?

PHILOSOPHIC ANTS:

A BIOLOGIC FANTASY [1]

"Incomprehensibility; that's what I say."—LEWIS CARROLL *(amended)*.

ACCORDING to a recent study by Mr. Shapley (Proc. Nat. Acad Sci , Philadelphia, vol vi, p. 204), the normal rate of progression of ants —or at least of the species of ant which he studied— is a function of temperature. For each rise of ten degrees centigrade, the ants go about double as fast. So complete is the dependence that the ants may be employed as a thermometer, measurement of their rate of locomotion giving the temperature to within one degree centigrade.

*   *   *   *   *   *   *

The simple consequence—easy of apprehension by us, but infinite puzzlement to ants—is that on a warm day an ant will get through a task four or five times as heavy as she will on a cold one. She does more, thinks more, lives more: more Bergsonian duration is hers.

There was a time, we learn in the myrmecine an-

[1] Read before the Heretics Club, Cambridge, May 1922.

nals, when ants were simple unsophisticated folk, barely emerged from entomological barbarism Some stayed at home to look after the young brood and tend the houses, others went afield to forage. It was not long before they discovered that the days differed in length. At one season of the year they found the days insufferably long; they must rest five or six times if they were, by continuing work while light lasted, to satisfy their fabulous instinct for toil. At the opposite season, they needed no rest at all, for they only carried through a fifth of the work. This irregularity vexed them: and what is more, time varied from day to day, and this hindered them in the accurate execution of any plans.

But as the foragers talked with the household servants, and with those of their own number who through illness or accident were forced to stay indoors, they discovered that the home-stayers noticed a much slighter difference in time between the seasons.

It is easy for us to see this as due to the simple fact that the temperature of the nest varies less, summer and winter, than does that of the outer air: but it was a hard nut for them, and there was much head-scratching. It was of course made extremely difficult by the fact that they were not sensitive to gradual changes in temperature as such, the change being as it were taken up in the altered rate of living. But as their processes of thought kept pace in alteration with their movements, they found it simplest and most natural to believe in the fixity and uniformity of their own life and its processes, and to refer all changes to the already obvious mutability of external nature.

The Wise Ants were summoned. they were ordered by the Queen to investigate the matter; and so, after consultation, decided to apply the test of experiment. Several of their numbers, at stated intervals throughout the year, stayed in and went out on alternate days, performing identical tasks on the two occasions. The task was the repeated recitation of the most efficacious of the myrmecine sacred formulæ.

The rough-and-ready calculations of the workers were speedily corroborated. "Great is God, and we are the people of God" could be recited out-of-doors some twenty thousand times a day in summer, less than four thousand times in winter; while the corresponding indoor figures were about fifteen thousand and six thousand

There was the fact; now for the explanation After many conclaves, a most ingenious hypothesis was put forward, which found universal credence. Let me give it in an elegant and logical form

 (1) It was well-known—indeed self-evident—that the Ant race was the offspring and special care of the Power who made and ruled the universe.

 (1.1) Therefore a great deal of the virtue and

essence of that Power inhered in the race of Ants. Ants, indeed, were made in the image of God.

(1.2) It was, alas, common knowledge that this Power, although Omnipotent and Omniscient, was confronted by another power, the power of disorder, of irregularity, who prevented tasks, put temptations in the way of workers, and was in fact the genius of Evil.

(2) Further, it was a received tradition among them that there had been a fall from the grace of a Golden Age, when there were no neuters, but all enjoyed married bliss; and the ant-cows gave milk and honey from their teats.

(2.1) And that this was forfeited by a crime (unmentionable, I regret to say, in modern society) on the part of a certain Queen of Ants in the distant past. The Golden Age was gone; the poor neuters—obligate spinsters—were brought into being; work became the order of the day. Ant-lions with flaming jaws were set round that kingdom of Golden Age, from which all ants were thenceforth expelled.

(2.2.1) This being so, it was natural to conclude that the fall from grace involved a certain loss of divine qualities.

(2.2.2) The general conclusion to be drawn was

that in the race of ants there still resided a certain quantity of these virtues that give regularity to things and events; although not sufficient wholly to counterbalance the machinations of the power of evil and disorder.

(2.2.3) That where a number of ants had their home and were congregated together, there the virtue resided in larger bulk and with greater effect, but that abroad, where ants were scattered and away from hearth, home, and altar, the demon of irregularity exerted greater sway.

This doctrine held the field for centuries.

     *   *   *   *   *   *   *

But at last a philosopher arose. He was not satisfied with the current explanation, although this had been held for so long that it had acquired the odour and force of a religious dogma. He decided to put the matter to the test. He took a pupa (*anglice* "ant's egg") and on a windless day suspended it from a twig outside the nest. There he had it swung back and forth, counting its swings. He then (having previously obtained permission from the Royal Sacerdotal College) suspended the pupa by the same length of thread from the roof of the largest chamber of the nest—a dome devoted to spiritual exercise— and repeated the swinging and the counting. The living pendulum-bob achieved the same daily number of oscillations inside the nest as outside, although it was full summer, and the foragers found the day quite twice as long as did the home-stayers. The trial was repeated with another pupa and other lengths of thread; the result was always the same.

It was then that he laid the foundations of ant science by his bold pronouncement that neither the combat of spiritual powers nor the expansion or con- traction of the store of divine grace had anything to do with the strange alteration of diurnal length; but that the cause of it lay in the Ants themselves, who varied with the varying of something for which he invented the word *Temperature,* not in a contraction or expansion of Time.

This he announced in public, thinking that a tested truth must be well-received, and would of necessity some day prove useful to society. But the conse- quence was a storm of protest, horror, and execration.

Did this impious creature think to overthrow the holy traditions with impunity? Did he not realize that to impugn one sentence, one word, one letter of the Sacred Books was to subvert the whole? Did he think that a coarse, simple, verifiable experiment was to weigh against the eternal verity of subtle and mysterious Revelation? No! and again a thousand times No!!

He was brought before the Wise Ants, and cross- questioned by them. It was finally decided that he was to abjure his heretical opinion and to recant in public, reciting aloud to the four winds of heaven: "the Ant is the norm of all"—

Μύρμηξ παντὸς νόμος.

He said it. But Truth stirred within him, and under his breath he muttered "Eppur si muove . . ." This was overheard, and he was condemned (loneliness being much hated and dreaded by ants) to a solitary banishment.

Later philosophers, however, by using this same pendulum method, were enabled to find that the movements of sap in plants differed in rate according to the length of day, and later discovered that the expansion of water in hollow stems also followed these changes. By devising machines for registering these movements, they were enabled to prophesy with considerable success the amount of work to be got through on a given day, and so to render great aid to the smooth working of the body politic. Thus, gradually, the old ideas fell into desuetude among the educated classes—which, however, did not prevent the common people from remaining less than half-convinced and from regarding the men of science with suspicion and disapproval.

*   *   *   *   *   *   *

We happen to be warm-blooded—to have had the particular problem faced by our philosophic ants solved for us during the passage of evolutionary time, not by any taking of thought on our part or on the part of our ancestors, but by the casual processes of variation and natural selection. But a succession of similar problems presses upon us. Relativity is in the air; it is so much in the air that it becomes almost stifling at times; but even so, its sphere so far has been the inorganic sciences, and biological relativity, though equally important, has been little mentioned.

We have all heard the definition of life as "one damn thing after another"; it would perhaps be more accurate to substitute some term such as *relatedness* for *thing*.

When I was a small boy, my mother wrote down in a little book a number of my infant doings and childish sayings, the perusal of which I find an admirable corrective to any excessive moral or intellectual conceit. What, for instance, is to be thought of a scientist of whom the following incident is recorded, even if the record refers to the age of four years?

I (for convenience one must assign the same identity to oneself at different ages, although again it is but a relative sameness that persists)—I had made some particularly outrageous statement which was easily proved false: to which proof, apparently without compunction, I answered, "Oh, well, I always ex*agg*-erate when it's a fine day. . . ."

The converse of this I came across recently in a solemn treatise of psychology: a small girl of five or six, in the course of an "essay" in school, affirmed that the sun was shining and the day was fine; while as a matter of fact it had been continuously overcast and gloomy: on being pressed for a reason, she explained that she felt so happy that particular morning that she had been sure it was a fine day.

If the weather can affect one's statements of fact, and one's emotions can affect the apparent course of meteorological events, where is the line to be drawn? What is real? The only things of which we have immediate cognizance are, of course, happenings in our minds: and the precise nature and quality of each of these happenings depends on two things—on the constitution and state of our mind and its train on the one hand; on the other hand upon events or relations between events outside that system. That sounds very grand; but all it means after all is that you need a cause to produce an effect, a machine to register as well as a something to be registered.

As further consequence, since this particular machine (if I may be permitted to use the odious word in a purely metaphorical sense), this mind of ours, is never the same for two succeeding instants, but continually varies both in the quantity of its activity and the quality of its state, it follows that variations in mental happenings depend very largely on variations in the machine that registers, not by any means solely upon variations in what is to be registered.

Few (at least among Englishmen) would dispute the thesis that food, properly cooked and served, and of course adapted to the hour, is attractive four times in the day. But to a large proportion among us, even sausages and marmalade at nine, or roast beef and potatoes on a Sabbath noon, would prove not only not attractive but positively repellent if offered us on a small steamer on a rough day. I will not labour the point.

We all know how the size of sums of money appears to vary in a remarkable way according as they are being paid in or paid out. We all know to our cost the extraordinary superiority of the epochs when our more elderly relatives were youthful. The fact remains that we are always prone to regard the registering machine as a constant, and to believe that all the variation comes from outside. It is easy to discount the inner variation in ourselves when we are seasick, or in others when they are old and reminiscent, but not only is this discounting sometimes far more difficult, it is sometimes not even attempted.

What, for instance, are we to say to those who profess to find a harmony in the universe, those to whom poverty and discomfort and hard work appear the merest accidents, to whom even disease, pain, loss, death, and disaster are "somehow good"? You and I would probably retort that we have a rooted dislike to discomfort, that we should most strongly deny that the loss of a friend or even of a leg was anything but bad, that a toothache was not damnably unpleasant. But I think that if they were philosophically inclined (which they probably would not be), they might justifiably retort that the difference between their universe and ours was due to a difference in their mental machinery, which they had succeeded in adjusting so that it registered in a different and a better way.

It is at least clear that something of the sort can happen in the intellectual sphere. To the uneducated, the totality of things, if ever reflected upon, is a compound of fog and chaos: advance is painfully slow, and interlarded with unpleasant falls into pits and holes of illogicality and inconsequence; to those who have taken the trouble to push on, however, an orderly system at last reveals itself.

The problem of the origin and relationship of species gave such mental distress to those zoologists of the first half of the nineteenth century who were conscientious enough to struggle with it, that many of them ended by a mental suppression of the problem and a refusal to discuss it further. The publication of Darwin's *Origin of Species* was to them what psycho-analysis is (or may be) to a patient with a repressed complex. Or again, no one can read accounts of the physicists' recent work on the structure of the atom without experiencing an extraordinary feeling of satisfaction. Instead of wallowing in unrelated facts, we fly on wings of principle; not only can we better cut our way through the jungle of things, but we are allowed a privilege that has universally been considered one of the attributes of Gods —the calm and untroubled understanding of things and processes.

"The Gods are happy.
They turn on all sides
Their shining eyes,
And see below them
The earth and men."

This being so, what is to prevent us from believing that, once certain adjustments are made in the mental sausage-machine, we shall discover that what we once found impossibly tough meat will pass smoothly through and become done up into the most satisfactory of sausages?   In other words, that the values are there if we choose to make them—an Euckenish doctrine which, for all that it arouses instinctive suspicion, may none the less be true.

But even when we have made all possible discounts of this kind, evolved the smoothest-running machinery, converted the raw and meaty material of being into every conceivable kind of tidy sausage, the fact remains that there are feats beyond the power of our machine—beyond its power because of the very quality of its being

We live at a certain rhythm in time, at a certain level of size and space; beyond certain limits, events in the outer world are not directly appreciable by the ordinary channels of sense, although a symbolic picture of them may be presented to us by the intellect.

When we are listening to the organ, sometimes there come notes which are on the border-line between sound and feeling: their separate vibrations are distinguishable and pulse through us, and the more the vibrations are separable, the more they are felt as mechanical shocks, the less as sound. However, we know perfectly well that all sounds as a matter of fact depend on vibratory disturbance, and that it is only some peculiarity of the registering machinery, in ear or brain, which enables us to hear a note as continuous.

Still more remarkable are the facts of vision. As I write I see the tulips in my garden, red against the green grass: the red is a continuous sensation; but the physicists appear to be justified in telling us that the eye is being bombarded every second with a series of waves, not the few hundred or thousand that give us sound, but the half-billion or so which conspire to illuminate our vision.

With sound, we alter the frequency of the waves and we get a difference of tone which seems to be merely a difference of more or less: but alter the frequency of light-waves, and the whole quality of the sensation changes, as when I look from the tulips to the sky. The change of registering mechanism is here more profound than the change in outer event.

Or again, to choose an example that depends more on size than rhythm, how very difficult it is to remember that the pressure of air on our bodies is not the uniform gentle embrace of some homogeneous substance, but the bombardment of an infinity of particles. The particles are not even all alike: some are of oxygen, others of nitrogen, of carbonic acid gas, of water vapour. They are not all travelling at uniform speeds; collisions are all the time occurring, and the molecules are continuously changing their rate of travel as they clash and bump.

We have only to look down a microscope to convince ourselves of the alteration in our experience that it would mean if we were to become sufficiently diminished The tiniest solid particles in fluids can be seen to be in a continuous state of agitation—inexplicable until it was pointed out that this mysterious "Brownian" movement was the inevitable result of impacts by the faster-moving molecules of the fluid. Many living things that we can still see are small enough to live permanently in such agitation; the longest diameter of many bacteria is but half a micron (a two-thousandth of a millimetre), and there are many ultra-microscopic organisms which, owing to their closer approximation to molecular dimensions, must pass their lives in erratic excursions many times more violent than any visible Brownian motion.

If we could shrink, like Alice, at the persuasion of some magic mushroom, the rain of particles on our skin, now as unfelt as midges by a rhinoceros, would at last begin to be perceptible. We should find ourselves surrounded by an infinity of motes; titillated by a dance of sand-grains, bruised by a rain of marbles; pounded by flights of fives-balls. What is more, the smaller we became, the more individuality and apparent free-will should we detect in the surrounding particles As we got still smaller, we should, now and again, find the nearly uniform bombardment replaced by a concerted attack on one side or the other, and we should be hurled for perhaps double our own length in one direction. If we could conceivably enter into a single inorganic molecule, we should find ourselves one of a moving host of similar objects: and we should further perceive that these objects were themselves complex, some like double stars, others star-clusters, others single suns, and all again built of lesser units held in a definite plan, in an architecture reminding us (if we still had memory) of a solar system *in petto*. If we were lucky enough to be in a complicated fluid like sea-water, we should be intrigued by the relations of the different kinds of particles. They would be continually coming up to other particles of different kinds, and would then sometimes enter into intimate union with them. If we could manage to follow their history, we should find that after a time they would separate, and seek new partners, of the same or of different species. Some kinds of the units, or people as we should be inclined to call them, would spend most of their existence in the married state, others would apparently prefer to remain single, or, if they married, would within no long time obtain divorce

We should be forcibly reminded of life in some cosmopolitan city like London or New York. If there existed a registrar to note down the events of these little beings' existence, and we were privileged to inspect the register, we should find that each had its own history, different from that of every other in its course and its matrimonial adventures.

If we were near the surface we should find that the outer beings always arranged themselves in a special and coherent layer, apparently to protect themselves against the machinations of the different beings inhabiting the region beyond; for every now and again one would seem to be pulled from the water and be lost among the more scattered inhabitants of the air.

If we could now revert to our old size, we might remember, as we listened to the scientist enunciating the simple formulæ of the gas-laws, or giving numerical expression to vapour-pressures and solubilities, that this simplicity and order which he enabled us to find in inorganic nature was only simplicity when viewed on a large enough scale, and that it was needful to deal in millions and billions before chance aberrations faded into insignificance, needful to experience molecules from the standpoint of a unit almost infinitely bigger before individual behaviour could be neglected and merged in the orderly average. And we might be tempted to wonder how the personal idiosyncrasies of our human units might appear to a being as much larger than we as we are larger than a molecule—whether kings and beggars would not fare alike, and all the separate, striving, feeling, conflicting personalities, with their individual histories, their ancestors, successes, marriages, friendships, pains, and pleasures, be merged in some homogeneous and simple effect, altering in response to circumstances, with changes capable of expression in some formula as simple as Boyle's or Avogadro's Law.

Almost more startling might be the effect of altering the rhythm at which we live, or rather at which we experience events.

If only I were Mr. H. G. Wells, I could make a mint of money by a story based on this idea of rhythm of living.[2]   Let us see . . . First there would be Mercaptan the distinguished inventor, who would lead me (lay, uninstructed, Watsonish me, after the fashion of narrators) into his laboratory.   There on the table would be the machine—all but complete: handles, coils of wire, quartz terminals, gauges of rock-crystal in which oscillated coloured fluids, platinum cogwheels . . . dot . . . dot . . . dot . . . dot. . . . He hardly dared to make the final connections, all clear and calculable though they were.   He had put so much of himself into it: so many hopes . . . fears . . . dots. . . .

Then there would be the farewell dinner-party— first the inventor's voice on the wireless telephone,

[2] The reading of this paper brought a string of informants eager to let me know that Mr Wells had already written a story on this theme   I was grateful to them for having caused me to read the *New Accelerator*, which by some strange chance I had managed to miss but Mr Wells's treatment is so wholly different from that which I have sketched that I feel no scruples in letting it stand: and, if amends are needed, at least I make him a present of the germ of a new tale, and so feel that honour should be satisfied.

summoning Wagrom the explorer, Glosh of the *Evening Post*, Stewartson Ampill the novelist, and the rest of our old friends: then the warm friendly light of the candles, the excellent port, the absence of women, the reminiscences, the asterisks, the. . . .

Mercaptan refuses to allow the rest to come into the laboratory, in case something should go wrong. He straps the machine on his shoulders, makes a final connection; his life processes begin to work faster, faster, ever faster. The first effect of course was a change of colour. The blue oblong of the window became green—yellow—orange—red Meanwhile each wave-length of the ultra-violet became blue, and itself ran down the gamut of colour. Then came the turn of the X-rays—by their dim light he groped about, till they too became relatively too slow for his retina. That ought to make him blind, of course—but no! Mr. Wells had thought that all out; and he came into a state of nearly maximum speed where he perceived a brilliant, phosphorescent light given out by all objects, generated by disturbances of a wave-length unimaginably, undiscoverably small Meanwhile he had passed through an amazing experience—he had heard the veritable music of the spheres! That had happened when in his acceleration he had, so to speak, caught up with the light-waves, until they were tuned to his ear's organ of Corti: and all that had been visible in his ordinary life was now to be appreciated by hearing Unfortunately, as his ears possessed no lens, this universal music was to him of course merely a hideous babel of sound.

At last, as the workings of his body approached the rapidity of light's own oscillations, he entered on a new phase—surrounded on every side by an ocean of waves which lapped softly against his body —waves, waves, and still more waves. . . .

He was in that region not unlike that from which life has escaped when it ceased to be infinitely little, a region in which none of the events that make up our ordinary life, none of the bodies that are our normal environment, have existence any more—all reduced to a chaos of billows ceaselessly and meaninglessly buffeting his being

"Mi ritrovai in una selva oscura."

Life is a wood, dark and trackless enough to be sure; but Mercaptan could not even see that it was a wood—for the trees.

Yet it was soothing: the very meaninglessness of the wave-rocking released one of responsibility, and it was delicious to float upon this strange etheric sea.

Then his scientific mind reasserted itself. He realized that he had magnified his rate of life and was consuming his precious days at an appalling speed. The lever was thrown into reverse, and he passed gradually back to what he had been accustomed to think of as reality.

Back to it; and then beyond it, slowing his vital rhythm. This time he was able by an ingenious arrangement to eliminate much of the disturbing

effect of his rhythm-change on his vision.   It was an
idea of which he was very proud: every alternate
light-wave was cut out when he doubled the capacity
of each process of life, and so on in automatic corre-
spondence.   As a result he was enabled to get a picture of the outer world very similar to that obtained
in the ordinary accelerations of slow processes that
are made possible by running slow-taken cinema records at high speed.   He saw the snowdrops lift their
matutinal heads and drop them again at evening—
an instant later; the spring was an alarming burst of
living energy, the trees' budding and growth of leaves
became a portent, like the bristling of hairs on the
backs of vegetable cats.   As his rate changed and
he comprehended more and more in each pulse, the
flowers faded and fell before he could think of pluck-
ing them, autumnal apples rotted in his grasp, day
was a flash and night a wink of the eye, the two
blending at last in a continuous half-light.

After a time ordinary objects ceased to be distinguishable; then the seasons shared the fate of day
and night.   The lever was now nearly hard over,
and the machine was reaching its limits.   He was
covering nearly a thousand of men's years with each
of his own seconds.

The cinema effect was almost useless to him now;
and he discarded this apparatus.   Now followed
what he had so eagerly awaited, something deducible
in general but unpredictable in all particulars.   As
the repeated separate impacts of the ether waves had

condensed, at his old ordinary rate, to form the continuous sensation of light, so now the events of nature coalesced to give new objects, new kinds of sensation. Especially was this so with life: the repeated generations seemed to act like separate repeated waves of light, blending to give a picture of the species changing and evolving before his eyes.

Other experiences he could explain less well. He was conscious of strange sensations that he thought were probably associated with changes in energy-distribution, in entropy; others which he seemed to perceive directly, by some form of telepathy, concerning the type of mental process occurring around him. It was all strange: but of one thing he was sure—that if only he could find a way of nourishing and maintaining himself in this new state, he would be able, as a child does in the first few years of life, to correlate his puzzling new sensations, and that when he had done this he would obtain a different and more direct view of reality than any he had ever obtained or thought of obtaining before.

As the individual light-waves were summed to give light, as the microcosm of gas-molecules cancelled out to give a uniformity of pressure, so now the repetition of the years coalesced into what could be described as visible time, a sensation of cosmic rate; the repeated pullulations of living things fused into something perceived as organic achievement: and the infinite variety of organisms, their conflicts and interactions, resolved itself, through the mediation of his sense-organs and brain at their new rhythm, into a direct perception of life as a whole, an entity with a pressure on its environment, a single slowly-evolving form, a motion and direction.

He put the lever to its limit: the rhythm of the cosmos altered again in relation to his own. He had an extraordinary sense of being on the verge of a revelation. The universe—that was the same; but what he experienced of it was totally different. He had immediate experience of the waxing and waning of suns, of the condensation of nebulæ, the slowing down and speeding up of evolutionary processes.

The curious, apparently telepathic sense which he had had of the mental side of existence was intensified. Through it, the world began to be perceived as a single Being, with all its parts in interaction. The shadowy lineaments of this being were half seen by his mental vision—vast, colossal, slowly changing; but they appeared only to disappear again, like a picture in the fire.

Strive as he might, he could not see its real likeness. Now it appeared benign; at its next dim reappearance there would be a feeling of capricious irresponsibility about it: at another instant it was cold, remote; once or twice terrible, impending over and filling everything with a black demoniacal power which brought only horror with it.

If he could but accelerate the machine! He

wanted to *know*—to know whether this phantom
were a reality, to know above all if it were a thing of
evil or of good· and he could not know unless he
could advance that last final step necessary to fuse
the rhythm of separate events into the sensation of
the single whole

He sat straining all his faculties: the machine
whirred and rocked. but in vain.   And at last, feeling desperately hungry, for he had forgotten to take
food with him, he gradually brought back the lever
to its neutral-point.

*   *   *   *   *   *   *

Of course, Mr. Wells would have done it much
better than this.

*   *   *   *   *   *   *

And then there would have to be an ending.
I think the newspaper man would take his opportunity to slink off into the laboratory and get on
the machine with the idea of making a scoop for
his paper; . . . and then he would put the lever
in too violently, and be thrown backwards His
head hit the corner of a bench, and he remained
stunned; but by evil chance, the handles of the machine still made connection with his body after the
fall.   The machine was making him adjust his
rhythm to that of light; so that he was living at an
appalling rate.   He had gone into the laboratory late
at night.   Next morning they found him—dead.

and dead of senile decay—grey-haired, shrivelled, atrophic.

Then of course the machine is smashed up; and Mr. Wells begins to write another book.

*   *   *   *   *   *   *

I have spent so much time in frivolous discussion of rhythm and size and commonplaces that I have not pointed out another fundamental fact of biological relativity—to wit, that we are but parochial creatures endowed only with sense-organs giving information about the agencies normally found in our own little environment.   Mind without the objects of mind is the very Chimaera bombinating *in vacuo*.

Out of all the ether waves we are sensitive to an octave as light, and some few others as heat.   X-rays and ultra-violet destroy us, but we know nothing about them until they begin to give us pain; while the low swell of Hertzian waves passes by and through us harmless and unheeded   Electrical sense again we have none.

Imagine what it would be for inhabitants of another planet where changes in Hertzian waves were the central, pivotal changes in environment, where accordingly life had become sensitive to "wireless" and to nought else save perhaps touch—imagine such beings broadcast upon the face of the Earth   With a little practice and ingenuity they would no doubt be able to decipher the messages floating through our atmosphere, would feel the rhythms of the Black Hamitic Band transmitting Jazz to a million homes, and be able to follow, night by night, the soporific but benevolent fairy-stories of Uncle Archibald. I wonder what they would make of it all. They would at intervals, of course, be bumping into things and people. But would touch and radio-sense alone make our world intelligible? I wonder. . . .

When we begin trying to quit our anthropocentry and discover what the world might be like if only we had other organs of body and mind for its assaying, we must flounder and bump in a not dissimilar fashion.

Even the few senses that we do possess are determined by our environment. Sweet things are pleasant to us: sugar is sweet: so is "sugar of lead"— lead acetate; sugar is nutritious, lead acetate a poison. The biologist will conclude, and with perfect reason, that if sugar was as rare as lead acetate in nature, lead acetate as common as sugar, we should then abominate and reject sweet things as emphatically as we now do filth or acids or over-hot liquids.

But I must pause, and find a moral for my tale; for all will agree that a moral has been so long out of fashion that it is now fast becoming fashionable again.

Every schoolboy, as Macaulay would say, knows William of Occam's Razor—that philosophical tool of admirable properties:—"Entia non multiplicanda praeter necessitatem."

We want another razor—a Relativist Razor; and with that we will carry out barbering operations worthy of another Shaving of Shagpat: we will shave the Absolute.

The hoary Absolute, enormous and venerable, grey-bearded and grey-locked—he sits enthroned, wielding tremendous power, filling young minds with fear and awe.

Up, barbers, and at him! Heat the water of your enthusiasm: lather those disguising appurtenances. See the tufts collapse into the white foam—feel the hairy jungles melt away before your steel! And at the end, when the last hair falls, you will wipe away the lather, and look upon that face and see—ah, what indeed?

I will not be so banal as to attempt to describe that sight in detail. You will have seen it already in your mind's eye: "or else" (to quote Mr. Belloc)— "or else you will not; I cannot be positive which." If not, you never will; if yes, what need to waste more of the compositor's time? But of him who forges that razor, who arms those barbers, who gives them courage for their colossal task, of him shall a new Lucretius sing.

BIBLIOGRAPHY

Belloc, H. "The Bad Child's Book of Beasts."
Bergson, H. "Time and Free-Will."
Carroll, L. "Alice in Wonderland."
—— —— "Alice Through the Looking Glass."
Clerk Maxwell. "Collected Papers."

Einstein. See Kant.

Hegel. See Einstein.

Kant. See Hegel.

Lear, E. "Nonsense Songs and Stories."

Lucretius. "De Rerum Natura."

Macaulay, Lord. "Essays."

Mee, A. "Children's Encyclopædia."

Meredith, G. "The Shaving of Shagpat."

Occam, W. de. "Opera Omnia."

Shapley. Proc. Nat. Ac. Sci., 6, 204.

Swift, J. "Gulliver's Travels."

Wells, H. G. "The New Accelerator."

Wheeler, W. M. "Ants" (Columbia University Series).

VI

RATIONALISM AND THE IDEA
OF GOD

GODS

Surprised by doubt, and longing but to know,
  I asked of men and books what God might be:—
  "An immanent spirit, clothed with the world we see"-
"A King of kings, ruler of all below"—
"Pure Love"—"A golden calf set up for show"—
  "A jealous chief and tribal sectary"—
  "Figment of fear and Man's servility"—
"The final Judge that dooms to joy or woe" . . .

I turned away; and found my God alone.
  God is the world—yet captive in our thought:
Our thought—when it the head of the world is grown:
  Love—with what love we to ourselves have taught.
The Soul must incarnate Divinity,
And God in each anew must builded be.

RATIONALISM AND THE IDEA
OF GOD

"Du gleichst dem Geist, den du begreifst."
—Goethe

"Nowadays, matters of national defence, of politics, of religion, are still too important for Knowledge, and remain subjects for certitude, that is to say, in them we still prefer the comfort of instinctive belief because we have not learnt adequately to value the capacity to foretell."—W. Trotter

NO one who has read Flaubert's *Tentation de St. Antoine* will be likely to forget that amazing procession of Gods, hundreds upon hundreds, in every diversity of form, defiling past the visionary Saint to topple over into the abyss of nothingness and be for ever destroyed—the doomed and outworn divinities of man's childhood and adolescence, put away as he came to maturity. "Man created God in his own image," wrote the irrepressible pen of Voltaire; and if it is not always true that Gods have been in his own image, but also in the image of animals and monsters, of embodied fears and hopes, it is indubitable that man has created God after God, only to throw them on the scrapheap as he outgrows them, like a child rejecting his old toys for new.

Indubitable—in a sense; indubitable that he has given each of them their peculiar and characteristic form, endowed this and that God with different qualities. But there is another part which he has not created, which he can only perceive, mould, clothe. The raw material of Divinity and its elemental attributes are given—man can but take it or leave it; and, what is more, it is difficult for him to leave it. It is given as the raw material and elemental attributes of life are given, and the evolutionary process can but take them. Man moulds and forms; but evolution has no more created living matter than he Divinity.

*   *   *   *   *   *   *

I propose, then, to lay down as my main point that the idea of God is an inevitable product of biological evolution, arising when the human type of mind first came into being, and taking shape and form as a definite God or Gods. That the Gods who thus arise, although of course they play a rôle in the affairs of the human species only, have a definite biological function. That the term God can still be properly and profitably employed to denote a certain complex of phenomena, with a certain function in human evolution.

What, then, do we mean by saying that the idea of God arises inevitably with the appearance of man upon the evolutionary scene? How can the appearance of man account for such a curious phenomenon?

With man, for the first time in the history of life upon the earth, an organism appeared capable of generalizing, of framing concepts, and of communicat-

ing them to his fellows. Through sense-organs and
brain, an organism reflects in its mind some of the
events of the world outside, creates some sort of a
microcosm over against the macroscosm   But the
animal with no more than associative memory can
at best create a haphazard microcosm, a mere cinema
record, and incomplete at that, of the most elementary organization; while all one can say of its power
of profiting by experience is that a certain primitive
plot is thus provided for the series of adventures
which make up the scenario.

With an organism like man, however, in which to
the faculty of associative memory there has been
superadded the power of framing concepts and of
accumulating experience by tradition, the picture is
altogether changed   The microcosm becomes more
highly organized; from rough-and-tumble cinema it
develops into an elaborate drama, whose plot is
knotted up in the same general way as that of the
great macrocosmic drama unrolling itself outside.
Microcosm images macrocosm more nearly, both in
its form and in its scope   As result of this, life is
for the first time enabled in man's person to frame
some general ideas of the outer world   Not only is
it enabled, it cannot help but do so   The outer world
is there; it impinges through man's sense-organs on
his mind, and his mind is so constructed that, if it
thinks at all, it must think in general terms.

For the first time, life becomes aware of something
more than a set of events; it becomes aware of a

system of powers operating in events. These powers (to use a general, and what is intended to be a noncommittal, term) are in constant action upon man's life. There is a power in the sun, a power in the storm, in the growth of crops, in wild beasts, in strange tribes, in the unrealized recesses of man's own heart; and in the course of his life man is brought into contact with these powers, which may act with him or against him. Man frames his own idea of these powers, and once that idea is framed, it exerts an effect upon the rest of his ideas, upon his emotions, upon his conduct. The more strongly the idea is held, the greater the effect.

But the idea may obviously be held and organized in many different ways. It is when the idea is organized in one particular way that we call it religious. We call it religious when on the one hand it involves some recognition of powers operating so as to underlie the general operations of the world; and, on the other hand, when it involves the emotions. It must involve the idea of the general powers operating in the outer world; so that an emotional reaction entirely limited to a single human being, or to beauty, or to a single event, is not religious And it must involve the emotional nature of man, so that a purely intellectual investigation of the powers in operation, or a purely practical response, a purely moral reaction to them, is again not religious.

*   *   *   *   *   *   *

In primitive societies, as the studies of a Frazer

or a Rivers have shown us, the whole of life is en-
meshed with religion, and there is scarcely an activity
of man which is not spun round with religious emotion and ritual. Very often the idea of God has not
in this stage been clearly formulated; there is simply
a notion of *power*, of mysterious influence, sometimes
partly crystallized round a primitive deity. Later,
however, the power became frankly anthropomor-
phic, and Gods came into being—many or one. Man
had projected the idea of that active agency he knew
best—human personality—into his idea of cosmic
powers.

Into the God thus fashioned there are always projected, to greater or less degree, the ideals of the community; and thus, at a certain stage of development,
we find definitely tribal Gods. Here the biological
function of Gods becomes extremely obvious. The
God, by his inspired prophets and priests, orders the
destruction of his rivals—the false Gods of neigh-
bouring tribes—or of his enemies, the members of
those tribes.

The people of the tribe, however the result may
have been brought about, do as a matter of fact find
themselves, all unconsciously, caught up in the system which they and their forefathers have made.
They have fashioned their God so that their inmost
life is joined to him. When they sin, they fear him;
when they look into their own hearts to take stock of
their ultimate ideals, they find that these are attached, through the impalpable but infinitely re-

sistant fibres of tradition, of childish memory and of education, to him; he is on their side against their enemies, so that their advantage is on the whole his.

Whatever, therefore, arouses the idea of God in their minds will send messages into every corner of their being And if they can be firmly persuaded that God wishes something done, the call will pull at their heart-strings and bring them to convinced and united action.

The most familiar example of this type of effect is to be found in the history of the Jews in the Old Testament.   But even to-day such tribal ideas are not extinct. an educated and charming lady said to me during the war—"I am convinced that if Jesus Christ were alive to-day He would be fighting on the side of the Allies." . . .

*   *   *   *   *   *   *

In our further analysis we must carefully distinguish between the outer and inner components of the idea of God.   The outer components are the powers acting upon man.   Some of these are inorganic— storms, winds, floods, the sun and moon; others are organic—wild beasts, pestilence, crops, and fruits, domesticated animals, others again are human—personal or national enemies, the community in which the individual lives And they may act upon man's body or upon his mind The sun warms his body, but makes an impression on his mind as well.   The practice of astrology shows what power can be exerted on the mind by quite imaginary properties of external reality. But, whatever we may think of these outer components, there they are, and they do affect us for better or for worse. Before such a heterogeneous assemblage as is constituted by the outer components can operate as a single idea, can deserve a single name such as God, they must be elaborately organized.

The contribution to the idea of God from within, from the mind of man himself, is its form; and this form is the outcome of a process of mental organization every bit as real as the physical organization occurring in the unborn embryo.

The essential thing about both is, as we have indicated, that unity should arise in spite of diversity, and the resulting entity—organism in the one case, organized idea in the other—should thus be able to act as a single whole.

The system of ideas which man holds concerning external powers may be thus organized by thinking of it in terms of magic, of "influence," manifesting itself in different ways in different operations of Nature; or in terms of personality, the manifestations of power being supposed to result from the activities of a being or beings more or less similar to ourselves; or it may be organized, as we shall see, on more scientific lines, by carefully pruning away all parts of it which are either definitely the mere product of our own imaginations, or else are not proven.

Thus what we have called the raw material of Divinity is given in the outer forces of nature, which not only act upon man as they act upon all organisms, but are by him perceived so to act in a way special and peculiar to man alone.

But, being so perceived, they are inevitably taken up into his mental life and made part of his mental organization. They are often perceived emotionally —to take the simplest examples, pestilence with horror, storm with fear, the growing of crops with gratitude. They are bound to enter into relation with his emotions, with his ideals and hopes, bound also to be in some degree generalized intellectually. When thus emotionally and intellectually built up so as to form a coherent and unitary idea, then only do they deserve the name of a God.

In parenthesis, let us make it quite clear that we are speaking of God and Gods as they operate in human affairs, as they can be classified by the anthropologist, analysed by the philosopher, experienced by the mystic. These have always been constituted as we have described—as a particular *idea* of the powers of nature, the cosmic forces taking shape through the moulding and organizing capacity of human thought, or, if you prefer it, as an interpretation and unification of outer and inner reality. The Absolute God, on the other hand, may be one—may, in fact, operate as a unitary whole in the same sense as this extraordinary product of the evolutionary process, this anthropological God; but we can never know it as such in the same sense as we know a person to be one.

This may be illustrated by a common fallacy—
the ascription of personality to God on the ground
that a purpose exists in the universe. Paley saw
proof of this purpose in adaptations among organisms. Modern theologians, driven from this position by Darwin, take refuge with Bergson in the fact
of biological progress. But this, too, can be shown
to be as natural and inevitable a product of the struggle for existence as is adaptation, and to be no more
mysterious than, for instance, the increase in effectiveness both of armour-piercing projectile and
armour-plate during the last century. The time has
gone by when a Paley could advance his "carpenter"
view of God; when a Fellow of the Royal Society
could be sure of general approval, as could D. Pront
in his Bridgewater Treatise, with a work entitled
*Chemistry, Meteorology, and the Function of Di-
gestion, considered with reference to Natural Theology,* or when a distinguished geologist like Buckland (almost foreshadowing later writers of a certain type on labour questions) could ascribe to a
Beneficent Designer the existence of Carnivora,
as a means to the increase of the "Aggregate of Animal Enjoyment," and solemnly open a sentence such
as "while each suffering individual is soon relieved
from pain, it contributes its enfeebled carcass to the
support of its carnivorous benefactors."

No—purpose is a psychological term; and to ascribe purpose to a process merely because its results
are somewhat similar to those of a true purposeful

process, is completely unjustified, and a mere projection of our own ideas into the economy of nature. Where we experience only phenomena of one order we cannot hope to reach behind them to phenomena of another order, or to the Absolute.

The ground is now cleared for our real investigation—our inquiry into the task which Rationalism has before it in finding how best what we have called the raw material of Divinity may be organized by the mind's activity, how best clothed with word or symbol to make it more the common property of mankind as a whole.

The current Christian conception of God is of a person who is also the creator and the ruler of the universe. This person has certain attributes—is omnipotent, omniscient, and somehow, in spite of all the unhappiness and squalor and cruelty in the world, all-loving He has personal qualities—he created the universe, and all that is in it; he takes pleasure in being worshipped; is displeased when men or women neglect him, or commit crimes or sins; takes pity on the follies and sufferings of man; and was so moved by them (albeit after a very considerable period had elapsed since man had first appeared upon the scene) that he sent his son into the world as a redeemer. (For simplicity's sake, I omit all reference to the complexities of Trinitarian doctrine, which, however important in distinguishing Christianity from other religions envisaging an omnipotent personal God, do not affect the essential point at

issue.) Further, he grants petitions, reveals himself
to certain chosen persons, and is enthroned in a somewhat elusive heaven, where he is (or will be after the
Day of Judgment—opinions seem to differ somewhat
on the subject) surrounded by the immortal souls of
the elect.

Now this view, or any view of God as a personal
being, is becoming frankly untenable. The difficulty
of understanding the functions of a personal ruler
in a universe which the march of knowledge is showing us ever more clearly as self-ordered and self-
ordering in every minutest detail is becoming more
and more apparent. Either a personal God is a ruler
without power, or he *is* the universe. In the former
case he becomes a mere fly on the wheel; in the latter
we revert to a frank pantheism, in which the idea
of a personal Being can no longer properly be up-
held. A personal creation of the world, in any reasonable sense of that term, is now meaningless except
for a hypothetical creation of the original substance
of the cosmos in the first instance. Creation of earth
and stars, plants, animals, and man—Darwin swept
the last vestiges of that into the waste-paper basket
of outworn imaginations, already piled high with the
debris of earlier ages. After the psychological insight which the last half-century has given us, miracles have ceased to be miracles, and have become
either delusions, or, more frequently, unusual phenomena for which a cause has not yet been found.
The immutability of the fundamental laws of matter

and motion, more particularly the grand generalization of the conservation of energy and the substitution by science of an orderly for a disorderly conception of nature, make it impossible to think of occasional interference by God with this world's affairs.
Accordingly the value of petitionary prayer falls to
the ground. Revelation and inspiration have resolved themselves into exceptional mental states, and
are no longer looked upon as a sort of telepathy between divine and human minds. If we reflect, we
see that all these intellectual difficulties in modern
theology arise from the advance of scientific knowledge, which has shown that the older ideas of God
were only symbolic, and therefore false when the attempt was made to give real value to them.

That being the quagmire in which traditional
Christian theology is floundering, it behoves us to
discuss the opposite side of the question, and to see
whether the very advance of science which has
seemed to exert only a destructive influence may not
have made it possible to build up new and sounder
conceptions of fundamental religious ideas.

We have already seen that the conception of God
always represents man's idea of the powers operating
in the universe; that it has two components—the
outer consisting of these powers so far as they are
known to man, the inner consisting in the mode in
which the conception is organized and the way it is
related to the rest of the personality. It is obvious
that both man's knowledge of the cosmic powers as

well as his method of organizing them in his mind can grow and change, and man's Gods can—and do —grow and change accordingly.

The growth of science in the last few centuries has radically altered our knowledge of the outer world. It has shown us, in the first place, a fundamental unity of all phenomena, however apparently diverse. It has shown us the inorganic part of the cosmos pursuing a direction—the progressive degradation of energy—which, if it is carried to its limit, will result in the extinction not only of life, but of all activity. It has next shown us the organic part, sprung from the inorganic but running a different course, ascending during evolutionary time to increasing heights of complexity and to increasing control over its inorganic environment.

Finally, we have the psychozoic or human portion —that minute fraction of the cosmos which yet is of a preponderant importance, since it definitely represents the highest level yet reached by evolutionary progress.   In this sphere mind is the dominant partner, biologically speaking, in the mind-matter partnership; evolution can begin to be conscious instead of fortuitous; and true *values* arise which, incorporated in ideals and purposes, exert an effect upon events.

As regards our own mental organization, psychological science has recently shown us the enormous importance of what we may call the extra-personal portion of our mind—all that which is normally subconscious, or has not been during our mental growth incorporated to form an integral part of our private personality. But this extra-personal part of the mind may from time to time irrupt into the personal, and does normally do so at some period of life. It is the merit of psychology to have shown the true nature of this relationship between personal and extra-personal, which was in the past a source of an infinity of mistaken ideas—revelation, inspiration, possession, direct communion with angels, saints, gods, or devils, and so forth.

Thus the powers operating in the cosmos are, though unitary, yet subdivisible; and, though subdivisible, yet related. There are the vast powers of inorganic nature, neutral or hostile to man. Yet they gave birth to evolving life, whose development, though blind and fortuitous, has tended in the same general direction as our own conscious desires and ideals, and so gives us an external sanction for our directional activities. This again gave birth to human mind, which, in the race, is changing the course of evolution by acceleration, by the substitution of new methods for old, and by introducing values which are ultimate for the human species; and, in the individual, provides, in the interplay of conscious and subconscious, unbounded possibilities of the invasion of the ordinary and humdrum personality of every day by ideas apparently infinite, emotions the most disinterested and overwhelming.

Still other light has of late years been thrown by psychology upon the inner component of the idea of God. Recent work has shown, for instance, that the mind, unless deliberately corrected and trained, tends to think in terms of symbols instead of along the more arduous paths of intellectual reasoning, tends to explain the unknown in terms of the known, tends accordingly to project the familiar ideas of its own personality as symbols for the explanation of the most varied phenomena. The science of comparative religion has shown us an early stage of religious belief in which but one idea held sway—the idea of a magical influence residing in all things potent for good or ill: the projection was so complete that no distinction whatever was made between the personal and the impersonal. Later, the idea of particular divine beings or Gods arose; and in early stages man still continued to project not only his own passions, but even his own form, into these divinities. The statement of Genesis that God made man in his own image is in reality an admission of the converse process. Still later, the divinity was purged of the grossness of human form and members, and, gradually, of characteristically human passions; but God remained personal, although the personality was now organized chiefly of ideals.

There is, however, no reason whatever to admit that personality is a genuine characteristic of any knowable God; but every reason to suspect that it is, as a matter of hard fact, merely another product of this property of projection so strong in the human mind.

On the other hand, an analysis of religious experience as a phenomenon, as something equally worthy of patient and scientific study as the gas-laws or the methods of evolution, shows that the powers which move in the universe, when organized by thought into a God, are apprehended by the majority of the great mystics and those to whom religious experience has been richly granted as in some way personal. Although, if our line of argument is valid, this will be partly due to a projection of the idea of personality into the idea of God, yet it is clearly in part due to the idea of God being organized by our mental activity to be of the same general type as is a normal personality—as something into which concepts of power, of knowledge, and of feeling and will all enter, with such interconnections between its parts that, like a personality, all of its resources are capable of mobilization at any one point.   It will be one of the great constructive tasks of psychology to ascertain just how such a conception is organized, and how it operates to produce the experiences, often of overpowering intensity and lasting value, which as a matter of record it often does.[1]

Put broadly and roughly, there are, then, three main accounts possible, or at any rate actually found in occidental civilization to-day, of the phenomena

[1] See W. James, *Varieties of Religious Experience;* E. Underhill, *Essentials of Mysticism.*

generally known as religious. The first is that of the out-and-out sceptic—that they are all illusions, imaginations of the childhood of the race. This is an extreme view which I do not feel called upon to discuss. The second is the view of almost every existing religious denomination in Europe—that God is a personal being. And the third is one, only just beginning to take shape, which I have endeavoured, with every consciousness of inadequacy, to outline—the account made possible by a radically scientific view of the universe.

Those who adopt the third attitude believe that the second is a purely symbolic and not very accurate presentation of certain fundamental facts, of which they are attempting to give what seems to them an account which is closer to reality. Before the scientific work of the last three or four centuries, it was impossible to attempt what we may call a realistic account of this nature, so that symbols were perforce adopted. In Christian theology man formulated a coherent scheme, which, however, was purely symbolic, to account for the facts we have just been considering. The chief feature in any such scheme must be the conception of the powers with which man feels himself in relation; and in this particular formulation his conception of these powers was that of a God who was also a person.

Now, the danger of symbols and symbolic thinking comes when the symbols are accepted for real, and taken as they stand for bases from which conclu-

sions shall be drawn.   The Christian theologians did
not hesitate—why should they, in their position?—to
use the personal nature of the Deity as one premiss
in a whole series of syllogisms, and to accept at their
full face value the conclusions which emerged from
these syllogisms.

If a personal God was ruler of the universe, then
he must be omnipotent, if truly divine, then omniscient, if worthy of worship, then all-wise.   He must
be capable of interfering with the course of events
by "miracles," of granting our prayers, of communi-
cating directly with us, of deciding our fate in after-
life.   From these conclusions yet further conclusions
were drawn.   If God revealed himself in the Bible,
then the Bible was "true" . . . with all that this in
its turn involved as to our beliefs concerning natural
causation, creation, our relations with God, or personal immortality.   The whole scheme was self-con-
sistent, and worked as well as many other human
schemes.   But what if the whole premiss, of God as
a personal being, ruler and father and judge—what if
this were not in fact tenable?   Then, of course, the
whole edifice itself would come toppling down   That
is what is actually happening to-day.   God, as personal ruler, is being slowly driven out of the universe, but returning as this organized idea of which
we have spoken.

Another cardinal point in the older systems has
always been its claim to possess a revelation of Truth
which is in some real ways complete and absolute.

This leads us on immediately to a subject of especial interest to us as rationalists—namely, the relation of religion to science and to free inquiry. Religious beliefs, if they are really believed with any conviction, will be to a greater or less extent dominant beliefs, because by their nature they concern the general relationship between man and his surroundings, which must bulk large in all our lives; and it is matter of common experience with what obstinacy and fanaticism they may be held. If therefore a system of religious belief includes the belief that it is revealed, and therefore true with a more ultimate and complete truth than the truths of observation or experiment, any fact or idea which conflicts with any part of the system will be inevitably treated not only as dangerous to the system, but as actually evil: and this tendency is reinforced by the craving of the average man for certainty, for intellectual satisfaction without undue intellectual effort. The cynic who said that beliefs are generally held with an intensity inversely proportional to the amount of evidence which can be adduced in their support was not wholly or only cynical.

Since, however, the progress of modern science, in addition to the discovery of many wholly new facts, has largely consisted in a proper investigation and a revaluation of the facts subsumed without full analysis into the symbolism of theology, the inevitable result has been for the two to find each other in constant antagonism. But be it noted that it is not science and religion which are in conflict, but science and a particular brand of religion.

The essence of science is free inquiry combined with experimental testing. The result is a body of knowledge, of fact, and explanatory theory, which can properly be regarded as established. By *established*, however, we do not mean that it is absolute or immutable—we expect addition and modification. But we also expect that, in the future as in the past, the additions and alterations will not involve the scrapping and rebuilding of the whole edifice, but that it will continue to be harmonious with itself, and to undergo a gradual evolution. This has been so even with such marked changes as the discovery of radioactivity, the new outlook in psychology, or the rediscovery of Mendelism—the new, after apparent contradiction, has been or is being harmoniously incorporated and organized with the old.

This in its turn implies that toleration should ever be encouraged by the scientist. Humility cannot be genuine if combined with unsupported dogmatic assertion: and the recognition that the ideas of revelation and divine personality are such dogmatic assertions brings a whole new outlook into being.

Putting matters in a nutshell, we can say that a system based on revelation or on the pushing of unsupported premises concerning the nature of God to their complete logical conclusions is bound to result in some degree of hostility to the pursuit of truth for its own sake; whereas a religious system basing

itself on scientific method, while it must resign itself
to being unable to produce a complete, ready-made,
and immutable scheme, however beloved of the
multitude (and indeed so beloved because it satisfies
a lower and more primitive mode of thinking only),
on the other hand can be assured that its knowledge
and effectiveness will increase, and that contradic-
tions will resolve themselves, provided that free inquiry, free speech, and tolerance are allowed and
practised. Attempts to reconcile the old formulation with the new facts and ideas, when not insincere,
are doomed to failure because the premisses of the
two systems are different.

In conclusion, we may perhaps point out some of
the bearings of such a change   In the first place, the
change in our conception of God necessitates the
stressing of religious experience, as such, as against
belief in particular dogma, or in the efficacy of special ritual.

Secondly, it emphasizes the need for tolerance and
enlightenment. The scientific view asserts not that
its knowledge is absolute or complete, but that, although relative and partial, it will indubitably continue to grow harmoniously along the general lines
already laid down.

Another change wrought by the inclusion of all
phenomena under one head and the banishment of
the supernatural is the inestimable advantage that
we thereby find the possibility of constructing a single general view of the universe for civilization. At

present there are two that matter—the orthodox religious and the scientific. The religious starts from the top, the scientific from the bottom; but the scientific has been creeping up, and now that it has begun to attack the problem of mind it will be able to drown the other out. Since the current religious formulation is only symbolic, it cannot become scientific; but since the scientific is based on the closest possible analysis of reality, it can become religious so far as it investigates the realities of religious experience.

Once it has done this, we shall be able to construct a *Weltanschauung* such as never before, with roots in the ordered reactions of inorganic matter, trunk strong with the steady progress of evolving life, and branches reaching up into the highest realities of the spirit. Union is strength; and it is one of the prime duties of educated men and women to see that the present duality and antagonism at the heart of what should be the central unity of civilization—of its most fundamental idea, its conception of the universe —should be terminated.

The new outlook will also interlock with the youthful science of psychology to produce great results. Much of what now is interpreted, by all save the few experts, in supernatural terms of the old theology will become intelligible as a product of the natural workings of that amazing thing, the human mind. We shall not have sects trying to exploit the normal dissatisfactions and disharmonies of adolescence in order to secure "conversions"; repressed tendencies

will not be thought to be the voice of a personal
Devil, nor neglected ideals the voice of a personal
God.   Irrational fear, to-day still the greatest enemy
of mankind and most potent annihilator of happiness, will, by comprehension of its curious mechanism
and its persistence, often transformed, from childhood to adult life, become amenable to treatment
and be made more and more to disappear.   Proper
analysis of mental processes such as repression, suppression, and sublimation will enable us to make
better use of our faculties, and deliberately to build
up treasures of spiritual experience now attainable
only by the lucky few in whom temperament and
circumstances accidentally conspire.

On the moral side, the idea that a Divine com-
mand has, at some remote period in the past, provided a fixed code, and the belief in the immutable
truth of certain dogmas—these will happily disappear.   Morals, like all else, not only have evolved,
but should evolve.   We shall find, for instance, that
no excuse will be left for the common horrified (and
horrible) views of sex, as of something inherently
hateful, of all its pleasures as involving sin; for it
will be realized that too much of the present attitude
is due to the projection of our own conflicts and com-
plexes, our own pruriences and pruderies, into what
might be innocent and joyous.   But this merits a
fuller discussion than we can here allot.

Again, if I had space at my disposal, I would write
of the changes in the position and constitution of re-

ligion brought about by changes other than those in religious beliefs themselves. Most important, of course, are the spread of education on the one hand, and the spread of the facilities for the most varied spiritual enjoyment on the other. If the people is educated to a point at which it can judge for itself, it wants no special priests or clerical mediators; its mediators are those who are specially fitted to unravel the intellectual, emotional, and moral difficulties of its own day and for all time—poets, philosophers, and men of science. The spread of facilities for reading, for seeing plays and works of art, and hearing good music, means of course that, whereas in ruder epochs the Church provided the principal way of psychological sublimation, now sublimation and spiritual refreshment can be achieved equally or more effectively (and every whit as religiously) without ever frequenting a "place of worship" or belonging to any denomination. This tendency towards fluidity and plasticity, towards many possibilities of sublimation instead of one, may by some be lamented. But, as a matter of fact, it is in full accord with all we know of biological progress.. Man has attained his position of biological pre-eminence simply and solely by virtue of the plasticity of his mind, which substitutes infinitude of potentiality for the limited range of actuality given by the instinctive reactions of lower forms. Humanity will always have some religion, and it will always be of the utmost importance to man, both as individual and as

species.   But the possibility of satisfying his religious tendencies intellectually, emotionally, and morally, without rigid creed, limited ritual, and iron-
bound code of morals, will mean the liberation of all
that is best in religion from too narrow shackles, and
the lifting it on to a plane where it may be not only
more free, but more rich.

It is the task of Rationalism to see that religion,
this fundamental and important activity of man,
shall neither be allowed to continue in false or inadequate forms, nor be stifled or starved, but made to
help humanity in a vigorous growth that is based on
truth and in constant contact with reality.

(For bibliography, see the end of the next essay)

VII

RELIGION AND SCIENCE:
OLD WINE IN NEW BOTTLES

GOD AND MAN

The world of things entered your infant mind
  To populate that crystal cabinet.
  Within its walls the strangest partners met,
And things turned thoughts did propagate their kind.

For, once within, corporeal fact could find
  A spirit. Fact and you in mutual debt
  Built there your little microcosm—which yet
Had hugest tasks to its small self assigned

Dead men can live there, and converse with stars:
  Equator speaks with Pole, and Night with Day:
Spirit dissolves the world's material bars—
  A million isolations burn away.
The Universe can live and work and plan,
At last made God within the mind of man.

RELIGION AND SCIENCE:

OLD WINE IN NEW BOTTLES

"In la sua volontade è nostra pace."
—DANTE

"Ye are the Gods if ye did but realize it."—CARLYLE.

"THE next great task of Science is to create a religion for humanity." So says Lord Morley in one of his essays. It is a striking saying, coming as it does from one in whom thought and action have been so intertwined, one to whom reason, not dogma, is the basis of morality, achievement, not emotion, its justification.

Let those words be my encouragement; for they challenge at the outset, and to my mind rightly, two of the most persistent difficulties that confront one who tries to write of the relations between Science and Religion. The man of science too often asks what science can have to do with what he brands as utterly and wholly unscientific; the religiously-minded man demands what gain can follow from contact with the cold and inhuman attitude of pure reason. To those questions I hope that this essay will provide a partial answer. Meanwhile I shall begin with a perhaps less ultimate but more pressing question. That question is asked by many men and women of to-day, who on the one hand feel as it were instinctively that religion of some sort is necessary for life, yet on the other are unable to do violence to their intellectual selves by denying the facts that reason and scientific inquiry reveal, or by closing their eyes to them.

The question, in briefest form, is this: "What room does science leave for God?"

To the savage, all is spirit. The meanest objects are charged with influence, the commonest actions fraught with spiritual possibilities, the operations of nature one and all are brought about by spiritual powers—but powers multifarious and conflicting. "Nature can have little unity for savages   It is a Walpurgis-nacht procession, a checkered play of light and shadow, a medley of impish and elfish, friendly and inimical powers." [1]

But with ordered civilization and dispassionate observation a network of material cause and effect invaded this spiritual domain. The mysterious influences, for example, believed to be inherent in springs and running rivers became personified, and, anthropomorphized as nymphs or gods, were removed into a seclusion more remote from practical and everyday life than their unpersonified predecessors. Later, they retreated still farther from actuality into a half-believed mythology, and then passed away into the powerlessness of avowed fairy-story or literary symbolism, while the rivers, perceived as the resultant of natural forces, were more and more har-

[1] W. James, '09, p. 21.

nessed to man's use.   So with the wind and the rain, the growth of crops, the storms of the sea.   So, in due time, with the thunder and the lightning, with earthquakes, eruptions, comets, eclipses, pestilences.

This process of liberating matter from arbitrary and mysterious power, of perceiving it as orderly and endowed with regularity of natural law, of bringing it more and more beneath human control, was, on the other hand, accompanied by what may be called a combined condensation and sublimation of the spiritual forces accepted by human faith.   They are built up from spirit to spirits, spirits to gods, gods to God.   But now it seems as if this condensation had reached its limit, and the sublimation could only go farther by resolving the one God into an empty name or the vaguest unreality.

We look back and see the Gods of early man, and are complacently prepared to believe that they were based in error, products of mental immaturity, to be relegated to limbo without regret.   But what about the present?   Why should we shrink from applying the same process to the God of to-day?

Is it then to be so with every God?   Is God only a personified symbol of our residuum of ignorance? Is to hold the idea of God in any form to be, as Salomon Reinach believes, in an infantile stage of human development, and must we with him define religion as "a sum of beliefs impeding the free use of human faculty"?

I think not; and I shall endeavour to justify my

belief to you, and to show that, albeit much alteration and a thorough revision of ideas is needed, the
term *God* has an important scientific connotation,
and further that the present stagnation of religion
can be remedied if, as has happened again and again
in biological evolution, the old forms become extinct
or subordinate, and a new dominant type is developed along quite fresh lines.

In any case the man of science must obviously, if
he face the problem at all, take up a scientific attitude of mind towards it.　He cannot say that there is
no such thing as religion; or try to whittle it away
by explaining that it is something else—a complicated fear, or a sublimated sex-instinct, or a combination of credulity and duplicity.　A thing, if it is a
thing at all, is never merely something else.　Nor
can he submit to the pretensions of those who assert
that it is too sacred to be touched, or that its cer-
tainties are greater than those of science.　No—he
must treat it for what it is—a fact, and a very important fact at that, in human history: and he must
see whether the application of scientific method to
its study—in other words, its illumination by the
faculty of pure intellect—will help not only our
comprehension of religion in the past, but its actual
development in the future.

He can study it in various ways.　He can use the
method of observation and comparison, collecting
and collating facts until he is able to give a connected account of the manifestations of religion and

of their past history; he can study it physiologically, so to speak, to see what part it plays in the body politic, and how that part may alter with circumstances; or he may seek to investigate its essence, to discover not only how it appears and what it does, but what it *is*.

Further, he must have some general principles to lean on in his search, principles both positive and negative. He must be content to leave certain possibilities out of account because as yet he cannot see how they can be connected with his organized scheme of things; in other words, he has to be content to build slowly and imperfectly in order that he may be sure of building soundly. This is the principle which we may call positive agnosticism.

This very fact has been in the past one of the great obstacles in the way of successful treatment of religion by science   One of the attributes of man is his desire for a complete explanation, or at least a complete view, of his universe, and this has been at the bottom of much doctrine and many creeds. But before Kepler and Newton, no truly scientific account could be given of celestial phenomena; before Darwin, none of Natural History; before the recent revival in psychology, none of the mind and its workings. In the second half of the nineteenth century, for instance, science could give an adequate account of most inorganic phenomena, and, in broad outline, of evolutionary geology and biology; but mind was still refractory. Accordingly, the philosophy of science was mainly materialist. But the common man felt that mind was not the empty epiphenomenon that orthodox science would have it; and he desired a scheme of things in which mind should be more adequately explained than it could be by science at its then stage of development. *Hinc illae lacrimae.*

To-day it is at least possible to link up, not only physics and chemistry and geology and evolutionary biology, but also anthropology and psychology, into a whole which, though far from complete, is at least organized and coherent with itself. If the seventeenth century cleared the ground for that dwelling-place of human mind which we call the scientific view of things, if the eighteenth century laid the foundations and the nineteenth built the walls, the twentieth is already fitting up some of the rooms for actual habitation.

There are certain other domains of reality which have not yet been properly investigated by science. Telepathy, for instance, and the whole mass of phenomena included broadly under the term spiritualism, are in about the some position with regard to organized scientific thought to-day as was astronomy before astrology's collapse, as was the study of electricity in the eighteenth century, or that of hypnotism in the middle of the nineteenth. What is more, the average man demands that phenomena of this order shall be included in his scheme of things. Science cannot yet do this for him, and accordingly the dwelling-place that we are building must still be incomplete; it is for those who come after to build the upper stories.

This cannot be helped. What we build, we must build firmly; on what is yet to be built, science cannot pronounce, except to say that she knows that it will be congruous with what has gone before.

What general principles, then, do we assume? We assume that the universe is composed throughout of the same matter, whose essential unity, in spite of the diversity of its so-called elements, the recent researches of physicists are revealing to us; we assume that matter behaves in the same way wherever it is found, showing the same mode of sequence of change, of cause and effect. We assume, on fairly good although indirect evidence, that there has been an evolution of the forms assumed by matter, that, in this solar system of ours, for instance, matter was once all in electronic form, that it then attained to the atomic and the molecular; that later, colloidal organic matter of a special type made its appearance, and later still, living matter arose. That the forms of life, simple at first, attained progressively to greater complexity; that mind, negligible in the lower forms, became of greater and greater importance, until it reached its present level in man.[2]

Unity, uniformity, and development are the three great principles that emerge. We know of no instance where the properties of matter change, though many where a new state of matter develops. The

[2] See Danysz, '21.

full properties of a molecular compound such as water, for instance, cannot be deduced at present from what we know about the properties of its constituent atoms of hydrogen and oxygen. The properties of the human mind cannot be deduced from our present knowledge of the minds of animals. New combinations and properties thus arise in time. Bergson miscalls such evolution "creative." We had better, with Lloyd Morgan, call it "emergent."

With mind, we find a gradual evolution from a state in which it is impossible to distinguish mental response from physiological reaction, up to the intensity and complexity of our own emotions and intellect. Since all material developments in evolution can be traced back step by step and shown to be specializations of one or more of the primitive properties of living matter, it is not only an economy of hypothesis, but also, in the absence of any evidence to the contrary, the proper conclusion, that mental properties also are to be traced back to the simplest and most original forms of life. What exact significance is to be attached to the term "mental properties" in such organisms, it is hard to say; we mean, however, that something of the same general nature as mind in ourselves is inherent in all life, something standing in the same relation to living matter in general as do our minds to the particular living matter of our brains.

But there can be no reasonable doubt that living

matter, in due process of time, originated from non-living; and if that be so, we must push our conclusion farther, and believe that not only living matter, but all matter, is associated with something of the same general description as mind in higher animals. We come, that is, to a monistic conclusion, in that we believe that there is only one fundamental substance, and that this possesses not only material properties, but also properties for which the word *mental* is the nearest approach. We want a new word to denote this X, this world-stuff; *matter* will not do, for that is a word which the physicists and chemists have moulded to suit themselves, and since they have not yet learned to detect or measure mental phenomena, they restrict the word "material" to mean "non-mental," and "matter" to mean that which has such "material" properties.

You will remember William of Occam's razor; "Entia non multiplicanda praeter necessitatem"; when we are monists in the sense I have just outlined, we are using that weapon to shave away a very unrestrained growth of hair which has long obscured the features of reality.

Holding to these principles, we must, until evidence to the contrary is produced, reject any explanation which proceeds by cataclysms, or by miracles; a miracle becomes (when not an illusion) simply an event which is on the one hand uncommon, and for which, on the other, there has been found no explanation.   Revelation too goes by the board—save a revelation which is simply a name for the progressive increase of knowlege and insight.

Last, but not least, we do not pretend to know the Absolute.   We know phenomena, and our systems, in so far as scientific, are interpretations of phenomena.

*   *   *   *   *   *   *

Religion has been defined in a hundred different ways.   It has been defined intellectually—as a creed; as myth; as a view of the universe; it has been defined emotionally as consisting in awe; in fear; in love; in mystical exaltation or communion.   It has been defined from the standpoint of action—as worship; as ritual; as sacrifice; as morality.   Matthew Arnold called it "morality tinged with emotion"; Salomon Reinach "a sum of scruples impeding the free use of human faculties."   Jevons makes the experiencing of God the central feature; and so on and so forth.   Is it possible to find any common measure for all these statements?   Would it not be better to unite with those who cut the Gordian knot by writing down all religion simply as illusion?   No.   For their point of view is meaningless.   Even illusions are, in themselves, facts to be investigated; and even illusions have a basis.

But it is not necessary to believe that it is an illusion; the knot may be untied.   Ritual, Creed, Morality, Mystical Experience—all these are mani-

festations of religion, but not religion itself. Religion itself is the reaction between man as a personality on the one side, and, on the other, all of the universe with which he comes in contact. It is not only
ritual, for you may have obviously non-religious ritual, as in a court ceremonial or a legal function: it
is not merely morality, for men may practise morality, the most austere or the most *terre à terre*, unin-
spired by anything that could remotely be called religious: it is not belief, for we may have beliefs of
all kinds, even to the most complex scientific beliefs
concerning the universe, which have yet no connection with religion: it is neither communion in itself,
nor ecstasy in itself, as many lovers and poets could
tell you.

But because it is a reaction of the whole personality, it must involve intellectual *and* practical *and*
emotional processes: and because man has the powers
of abstraction and association, or rather because his
mind in most cases cannot help making associations
and abstractions, it follows that it will inevitably
concern itself, consciously or subconsciously, with all
the phenomena that it encounters, will try to bring
them all into its scheme, and will try to unify them
and frame concepts to deal with them as a whole.

Some men will be more concerned on the emotional, others on the intellectual, others again on
the moral side: but it is impossible to separate any
one of the three aspects entirely from the others.

We will begin with and treat mainly of the intellectual aspect of the problem, the credal side. For one thing, science has more direct concern with it than with the others; for another, more continuous and startling alterations have had to be made in it; and finally, the actual problem is there felt most acutely at the present moment.

What, then, is the problem? In the terms of our definition of religion, it is in its most general terms as follows: Man has to live his life in a world in which he is confronted with forces and powers other than his own. He is a mere animalcule in comparison with the totality of these forces, his life a second in comparison with their centuries. By his mental constitution, he of necessity attempts to formulate some intelligible account of the constitution of the world and its relation to himself—or should we rather say in so far as it is in relation to himself?—and so we have a myth, a doctrine, or a creed.

At the present moment, as we have already seen, there appears to be an irreconcilable conflict between orthodox Christianity and orthodox Natural Science. The one asserts the existence of an omnipotent, omniscient, personal God—creator, ruler, and refuge. The other, by reducing ever more and more of natural phenomena to what we please to call natural laws—in other words, to orderly processes proceeding inevitably from the known constitution and properties of matter—has robbed such a God of ever more and more of his realm and possible power; until finally, with the rise of evolutionary biology and psychology, there seems to be no place any more for a God in the universe.

Stated thus, the opposition is complete. But let us return on our footsteps, and trace for one thing some of the history of religious beliefs, for another re-investigate, from a slightly unusual standpoint, the actual knowledge of the Universe which science has given us.

Man has developed: in early stages, his physical and mental capacities developed; in later stages development has been mainly restricted to his traditions, ideas, and achievements. As part of his development, his religious ideas have altered too.

At the beginning, he appears to have no ideas of a God of Gods at all—merely of influences and powers, obviously (he would say) inherent in the forces of Nature, magically inherent in certain objects and actions—fetishes and incantations. He seems scarcely to have been conscious of himself as an individual, or of the full distinction between self and the external world.

Later, perhaps as the idea of his own personality grew, he began to ascribe a more personal existence to the forces with which he came into contact, and so to turn them more and more into beings that can properly be called Gods: polydaemonism arose and in its turn gave place to polytheism.

But while rigid custom was at first the only morality, and each external power and each human activity was regarded separately, later the rise of civilization led to a modification of custom, to a reference of action and belief to the standards of pure reason, and to an attempt at unification. Once this occurred, and equally so whether the attempt at unification had an intellectual or a moral basis, polytheism was doomed. Its downfall has been often described; the reasons for it are suggestively put by Jevons in his little book, "The Idea of God." It passes through a stage where one among the gods is pre-eminent: but finally even that does not suffice, and in its place arises a monotheistic creed.

Monotheism may start as a purely local or tribal affair—my one God against yours. It may not only start, but long continue so. Readers of Mr. Bang's collection of startling German war-sayings will remember the superbly national prayer of the Prussian pastor who addressed his God (I quote from memory) as "Du, der hoch über Cherubinen, Seraphinen, und Zeppelinen ewig trönst." (J. P. Bang, *Hurrah and Hallelujah*. London, 1916.) But this idea, too, is self-contradictory, and merges into that of one God for all men. The primitive anthropomorphism which had invested the first vague and mysterious spirits with human parts and passions, human speech and thought, also fell into gradual desuetude. It was kept up as a symbol, or because of the difficulty of describing a God except in terms human individuality, but its literal truth was deliberately denied. God became different from and more than man—omnipotent, omniscient, with no parts, with no limitations: but he retained personality—in other words, a mental or spiritual organization of the same general kind as man's, however superior in degree. With time, the divine personality became compounded more and more of man's ideals instead of his everyday thoughts and attributes. And thus and that God remains. He has created everything: he is in some sense immanent in the world, in some sense apart from it as its ruler—you take your choice according to your philosophic preferences. Beyond that, organized religious thought has not gone; and now it finds itself fronting science in an impasse.

That, very briefly and roughly, is how man's idea of God has developed. But how have man's knowledge and ideas of the natural universe developed? What has Science to say to the impasse?

Man has to deal with three great categories of phenomena—the inorganic, the organic, and the psychic. In the inorganic, chemistry first and then physics have given us a picture whose broad outlines are now familiar. There is but one type and store of energy in Nature, whether it drives a train, animates a man, radiates in heat or light, inheres in a falling stone. There is but one substance. All bodies of trees, of men, rivers and rocks, the clouds in the air and the air itself, precious stones and common clay—all can be resolved into a limited number of elements. And these elements in their turn can be resolved into combinations, differing, it appears, only

quantitatively from each other, of electrical charges;
so that at the last all matter is one, and becomes perhaps indistinguishable, or at least inseparable, from
energy.   There is no personal operator for particular
happenings; the lightning and the volcano are the
inevitable outcome of the material constitution of
things, equally with the form and colour of a pebble
and with the fact that it will drop to the ground if it
is let fall.   All is impersonal order and unity

There is, however, one other great fact about the
system of inorganic matter   The energy contained
in it tends to be degraded, as the physicists say—in
other words to become less readily available.   There
is available energy in moving matter.   There is po-
tential energy in all matter, dependent upon whether
it can be set in motion   But if the sea were to cover
the whole surface of the globe, it would be impossible
to extract energy from running water as we do now,
because no water would be running.   So too heat is
energy; but it is only available when it can flow,
when there are hotter and colder bodies.   The law
under which transformations of energy operate has
now been investigated, and it has been established
that in every energy-transaction a certain modicum
goes to waste as unavailable heat, so that, unless some
at present unforeseen change occurs, the last state of
the universe, considered as a purely physico-chemical
mechanism, will be one of death, of inactivity, with
all matter at a uniform low temperature and the
whole stock of energy locked up and unavailable

in this sea of tranquillity. True for one thing that an almost inconceivable number of millions of years must elapse before this "death of matter" is realized; and for another that we are unable to understand how such a progressive degradation could have been in operation from all eternity. We must not expect complete knowledge within a few years or a few centuries; but even if the beginning is veiled—for there is no more evidence for a "creation" than for (say) a rhythmic reversal of the direction of energy-availability—and if it is always possible that some unforeseen change in the process should occur before the whole runs down, yet it is a fact (and we are resolved to be agnostic save about facts) that, here and now, a direction is to be observed in the evolution of inorganic matter, by which natural operations are tending to become less active, and the amount of available energy is diminishing. If it continues indefinitely, first life, and later on all activity and change whatsoever will cease. There is a tendency towards death and towards unchanging inactivity.

The next great category is that of the organic, of living matter. We have to consider its origin and later history So far as constitution goes, living matter is merely a special and highly complicated form of ordinary matter; and there can be no reasonable doubt that it has originated naturally from non-living matter.

While the *main* direction of the inorganic has been towards degradation of energy, it has shown another subsidiary direction towards the production of more and more complex forms of matter. If our general ideas are correct, there must have been a time when matter in our ordinary sense of the word did not exist—there can have been no atoms, only free electrons. From this state, there evolved one in which the various electron-systems that we call atoms first appeared; later still, atoms could join with atoms to produce molecules. Leaping over vast periods, we would come to the time when radiation had brought the temperature of the earth surface below 100 degrees centigrade; water then could form from steam and solution occur. Through solution, all soluble elements, which would otherwise remain locked in the inactivity of the solid state, are enabled to enter upon a new phase of mobility, of chemical life, as we may say. Only in water could colloid carbon compounds first be built up, and only from such substances could life originate.

Living substance, or at least much of it, must be formed of molecules containing thousands of atoms, each atom in its turn a system of circling electrons. Here already is a vast increase of complexity: it remains to be seen whether the same tendency is perpetuated later.

The evolutionary concept is to biology what the doctrine of the conservation of energy has been in the physico-chemical sciences—an indispensable preliminary to proper methods of attack. But while great stress has been laid on the various *methods* by which evolution may be supposed to have taken place—natural selection, Lamarckism, orthogenesis and the rest—biology has concerned herself comparatively little with the *form* of the process in itself. But it is here that evolution becomes of value to us in our present search; for once more we become 'aware of a direction. Partly from the direct evidence of palaeontology, partly from indirect evidence, but along many converging lines, we can form an idea of this direction which in broad outlines is unassailable.

During life's existence on earth—a period to be reckoned in hundreds and probably in thousands of millions of years—there has been an increase in various of its attributes. But just as in the inorganic world electrons and atoms still exist as such side by side with molecules, so also the earlier types of living matter continue to exist side by side with the later. The increase is not therefore seen uniformly in all forms at once, but is most easily observed by studying the *maximum* level attained. Size, for instance, is one of these attributes; and whereas to-day all variations are to be found between ultra-microscopic disease-germs and vast organisms like whales and elephants, there has been a gradual steadying increase (tending to a limit) in the size of the *largest* organisms existing at any one period.

If we confine ourselves for the moment to the material side, we find that the directional change in organic evolution can be reduced to this—to an increase of the control exercised by living matter over the environment, and of its independence of the environment—two reciprocal aspects of a single process. When we look more closely into the means by which this has been achieved, we shall see an increase of the maximum not only in size, but in complexity, in length of life, in efficiency of particular organs, in co-ordination of parts and general harmony, in improvement of sense-organs, and, continuing even after other tendencies have reached their limits, in brain-size and consequently in complexity of mode of reaction and behaviour.

If we turn to the psychological side, we find that there has been an increase in the intensity of mental process. This is apparent in all aspects of mind, on that of emotion equally with that of knowledge, of volition equally with that of emotion. To be an amoeba or a worm is to live a life almost without windows. Perfection of sense-organs makes it possible for life to be aware of the different types of outer events, whilst memory and, later, associative memory give the possibility of understanding their history. In higher forms volition can be maintained for longer and longer intervals, can attain greater intensity, and can fix itself upon ever more and more distant objects. With depth of feeling comes also differentiation, so that finally we find in ourselves the possibility of organizing various blends of the simple emotions into the compound emotional forms such as reverence and admiration, called *sentiments* by McDougall.

Biologically speaking, therefore, the direction observable in mental evolution is again towards increased control and increased independence; by mental and cerebral improvement there is introduced a greater accuracy and a greater range of control, as well as better adjustment between organisms and environment, than would be otherwise possible to the same bodily organs.

The direction of life may therefore be roughly summed up in the two words "more life"—more both in quantity (have not both land and air been colonized during evolution?) and also in quality. More matter has been stolen from the lifeless and embodied in the living; and the living begins to be less helpless in face of the lifeless.

The direction of living matter is thus in many ways opposed to the direction to be seen in inorganic matter; yet not only has the organic arisen from the inorganic, but its direction continues one direction already traceable before the appearance of life.[3]

Finally, we come to the psychological aspect of the universe. We have already touched on it in connection with biology, and found that in many ways at least the development of mind follows the same lines as that of living matter, and helps forward the general trend of life.

[3] See Danysz, '21.

But finally a kink occurs, a critical point similar to that seen at the origin of living from non-living matter.   There the attributes of living matter which mark it off from inorganic matter become dominant —its capacity for self-reproduction, its tendency to organization.   The colloid carbon compound had been the highest known independent unit; from now on this place was taken by the organism.

In exactly the same way, in the final stages of evolution (as witnessed abundantly by fossil mammals) complexity of purely bodily organization had reached a limit, and survival, as is evidenced by increasing size of brain, came to be determined more and more by mental qualities.   Finally the curve of mental development caught up with that of body, and intersected it: mind became the dominant factor in the new type of organism, and in the subsequent history of the evolutionary process.   The *organism* ceased to be the highest unit, and gave place to the *person*, or self-conscious individual with organized mind.

This new critical point was reached when man arose; many authors recognize it for what it is, the beginning of a new era, by christening the subsequent geological period the Psychozoic.   That period, geologically speaking, has not yet run but a tiny span; and we are no more entitled to think that we have reached or even imagined the possibilities of its future evolution than we should have been entitled to regard the possibilities of purely biological evolution as having been exhausted after the far longer period needed to give rise to a coral polyp or a jelly-fish as highest existing types of organism. Even man as a biological species is in his infancy, not to speak of other psychozoic types that may be waiting in the womb of time.

But what are the characteristics of this new phase? In the first place, mind has become self-conscious; thus the evolutionary methods of psychozoic organisms may become conscious, and they come to direct their own evolution instead of having their destinies shaped by the blind forces of natural selection.

In most respects the same direction as before is pursued, but new methods are introduced. The rate of change, of movement in that direction, is accelerated; and the possibility is given of eliminating a vast deal of waste. A watchmaker sends out very few defective watches: why? because he makes his watches on a preconceived plan. Even when an improvement in watch construction is introduced, he can draw up his plan beforehand, and at the worst, waste only time and paper, instead of metal and far more time. Ideas do not need to be embodied before selection can act upon them; thus an increasing amount of evolutionary change will take place through the natural selection of ideas than through the older and far more wasteful process, natural selection of individuals and species.

Finally, values appear upon the scene. If we could ask a wild animal such as a fox what gave value to its life, and it could answer us, it would doubtless say food, sleep, comfort, hunting, sexual pleasure, and family companionship. But it cannot answer; nor can it know the value of what it pursues, but only appreciate the result. Strictly speaking, values do not exist for it. However, even if we allow ourselves to speak of values in the life of pre-human organisms, we see immediately that wholly new values are introduced after the critical point.

Putting it summarily, we can say that, with the rise of mind to dominance, various activities of mind come to be pursued for their own sake, to have value in themselves. Our life is worth living not only for the sake of eating and drinking, sleeping, athletics, and sexual pleasure. There is a value attached to knowledge for its own sake, apart from the possible access of control that it may bring. But this is new, a property of man alone; not even Athena's owl will exert itself through laborious years to understand celestial mechanics or physiology. The highest anthropoids do not attempt to create works of art, which for man come to have value in themselves. Natural beauty comes to have its value too; a cow (so far as known!) does not interrupt the business of its life to admire the sunset, whereas men may and do. Behaviour also is implicated; with the entry upon the scene of that practically unlimited number of possible reactions which give us what we call free will and choice, there comes a conviction that some modes of action are higher than others;

and so a scale of moral values comes into being.[4]

Nor is it merely that values, in the strict sense, are created; nor that new values come into being. But with the enlargement of mind and its more perfect organization, there arises a new method of appraising values, and so a new type of value altogether. I mean of course the so-called *absolute values*. Absolute values are never absolute in the sense of absolute completeness; they are relative to two things—to external reality and to our mental powers and organization.[5] They are abstractions; we generalize the value in our minds, and at the same time raise it to the highest pitch of intensity we can. An interesting point arises from this way of thinking. Apart from the guarantee of our own convictions, the observable direction of living nature is our guarantee of right: or one had better say that it is at once the guarantee and the touchstone of our convictions. But two things may be moving in the same direction, and, if one be moving much slower than the other, the slower may impede the faster; a pedestrian procession making eastward along Fleet Street

[4] See Haldane, '21; Thouless, '23

[5] A confusion of thought easily arises here. It may be absolutely true that 2 and 2 make 4, we may be absolutely right in certain cases to tell a lie, or may find an expression of absolute beauty in some one lovely thing. But we may grow to find that same thing aesthetically unsatisfying, we can imagine a state of society in which it would never be right to lie; while our correct knowledge of elementary arithmetic is something very partial and incomplete considered in relation to mathematical truth as a whole.

will hold up the life of the city for a time, and cows walking along railways are treated as obstacles by trains proceeding in the same direction So it comes about that much that was once progressive in organic evolution has become an obstacle or a drag to psychozoic evolution; it is *relatively* retrogressive, and, from our present standpoint, bad. To take the simplest and most fundamental example: evolution by blind natural selection was the method of progress for organisms below man. Unceasing struggle and courage was the chief factor in producing the grandeur and strength of the lion, the swiftness and grace of deer, the brilliance and lightness of the birds. But if the same end can be obtained both more quickly and more bloodlessly by new methods, then the old stands condemned. Here lies the key to the problem propounded by Huxley in his Romanes Lecture—the problem of man's relation to the rest of the cosmic process, at once sprung from it by gradual generation and separated from it by an absolute and unbridgeable chasm, at once one with it and in deadly combat with it and all its ways.

Our mode of envisaging the problem illuminates it, and shows it as inevitable and intelligible instead of insoluble and tormenting; and illuminates too many other minor problems of good and evil But all this is a side-issue: *revenons à nos moutons*

Unknown, or neutral, or hostile power: a movement similar in direction to the direction in which history on the whole shows we are moving, and to that which we desire with our highest aspirations, but operating blindly; an acceleration of that movement by the coming of mind to biological predominance, with certain consequent minor changes in direction by major changes in speed and in methods. Three tendencies, but all founded in one unity, and each arising out of the other—that is the picture drawn for us by the present state of science. In this sense, and in this only, can it be said that "all things work together for righteousness."

One word on an important side-issue—the problem of evil in man, of stagnancy and degeneration in organic evolution. Degeneration often does occur —a reversal, in other words, of the main tendency. But the positive fact remains that the *maximum* level is progressively raised, and that we find that stagnation of development and even sometimes degeneration have been factors indirectly helping on the main direction.

We must accept the positive main direction for what it is—an external sanction of faith; confess that we do not understand the detailed working of the whole, but see in the change of methods brought about by the rise of mind a hope that we shall gradually learn at least to dispense with much waste and evil and degeneration in the further course of evolution.

This main direction gives us cause for optimism. The exceptions to it temper that optimism. But the direction is there.

As we shall see later, we may either call the sum of the forces acting in the cosmos the manifestations of God, who in this case must be the Absolute God, and unknowable except through these manifestations. Or we may confine the term God to its anthropological usage, as denoting the objects of human religion, in which case we must admit that the term God as understood by man is constituted by *man's idea of* the forces acting in the cosmos, so that not only are these forces involved, not only a possible Absolute God behind them, but also the organizing power of human mind.

I wish you here to agree to my adopting the second alternative and giving the name of God to the sum of the forces acting in the cosmos as perceived and grasped by human mind. We can therefore now say that God is one, but that though one, has several aspects. There is one aspect of God which is neutral to us, in a way hostile, mere Power operating in the vastness of the stellar universes, apprehended only as orderly, tending in a direction which appears to be in the long run inimical. It is to this aspect of God that Mr. Wells has given the name of the Veiled Being—a somewhat primitive term for a true idea. There is another aspect, which is the one seen operating in that sphere which comprises the whole of life upon this earth—a sphere infinitesimal in relation to the whole, yet still vast in relation to ourselves. This aspect of God is our refuge and guarantee, for here we find our assurance that our human life is a part of a whole that is not antagonistic, but moves in the same general direction as do our history and our aims. There does exist, in Matthew Arnold's words, "a power, not ourselves, that makes for righteousness" And this second aspect is not wholly separate from the first, in spite of its difference of direction; for the first is its parent, physically and temporally, and the direction of biological progress is the continuation of a line of development marked out, within the opposed inorganic direction, even from the first.

Next, there is a more immediate and more often demanded assurance that we, as individuals or as single communities in space or time, are at one with humanity as a whole. Here it is that we look to the third aspect of God, which enshrines the directive forces operating in man. These directive forces are our instincts, our needs, our values, our ideals. When those are harmonized with each other and with the outer world by reason and experience, they form a power which we can see has been directive, normative in the past, and will continue to be so in the future. It alters with man's development; but after a first rudimentary phase, its main outlines, its type of organization remain the same, for man's instincts and ideals do not greatly change, and their harmonization with each other and with experience will generally proceed in the same broad way. Although in a sense this aspect is the smallest, as comprising the smallest physical field, yet in another it is the largest, since man's ideals are in themselves unlimited, non-finite; and the values involved, to our present type of mind, appear ultimate. This third aspect of God is again historically the offspring of the second, and through the second of the first.

Matter, life, mind—this is the simplest classification of phenomena. By means of processes analogous to obtaining a resultant by the parallelogram of forces, we can obtain a resultant of material operations in general, vital operations in general, and mental operations in general, numerous and varied in direction though they be. Life is the link between the other two. Living matter is so definitely one with non-living matter, not at all obviously one with mind; yet the direction of living matter is obviously similar to that of mind, not at all obviously one with that of non-living matter.

*   *   *   *   *   *   *

It is a simple fact that the conception which man has of the universe and its relation to himself exercises important effects upon his life A name therefore is needed for this anthropological phenomenon. *God* is the usual name applied, and we shall retain it in default of another, premissing that the word, like many similar general terms—"love," or "life," or "beauty," say—can be defined and applied in many ways, and that we apply it here in a particular and perhaps somewhat novel sense.

God in this sense is the universe, not as such, but so far as grasped as a whole by a mind, embodied in

an idea, [6] and in consequence capable of influencing
that mind, and through it the whole course of events.
It is not grasped as a mere sum of details, but, however vaguely and imperfectly, as a single idea, unitary
in spite of its complexity.   Nor is it the universe in
itself, but only so far as it has been thus grasped by
mind.   There exists no other meaning of the term
which, on analysis, is found to convey anything, or
at least anything scientific or comprehensible, to us
We may reason that there is an Absolute God behind
the universe and our idea of it.   But we have no
proof of this statement, and such an Absolute God is,
as Spencer pointed out, an Unknowable, and accordingly no concern of ours.   That part and these aspects of the universe which have been grasped by us
may prove to contain the key to many of our difficulties; meanwhile we can only be humble and admit
that our idea of God, even in this restricted sense, is
still extremely incomplete: and in this sense there
is a God far greater than our present idea and knowledge of God, only waiting to be discovered.

That which it is essential to establish is our way of
looking at the problem   The universe does come into

[6] It is interesting to note that a scientific treatment of the
problem may force an author almost unwittingly to similar conclusions. For instance, in Jevons' book ('10) the term "God"
hardly occurs at all, whereas the phrase "the idea of God" is to
be found on nearly every page If, as we are urging, God as
efficient agent in the world and as reality in contact with human
beings *is* outer world organized as idea, the reason for such peri-
phrasis at once appears.

relation with our minds, and there, owing to the way it and our minds are organized, generates an idea which exerts an influence upon us.

The external basis of the idea of God is thus constituted by the forces operating in the universe. The universe is a unitary whole, greater and more powerful than ourselves, and its operations have resultants in certain main directions—these are phenomena which we constatate like any other phenomena. They, and that other phenomenon of our contact with the Universe and our exposure to the play of its forces, give us our objective knowledge of God. The rest of our idea of God, the inner component, depends upon the mode of action of our minds.

So far, then, we have shown that recent advance in science, particularly in our understanding of evolution, has enabled us to give a more objective account than ever before of what is involved in the concept *God*, and so to pave the way for a consensus of thought on the question.

It will be observed that there is no idea of personality implicit in this conception of God—God may or may not possess personality. It will be for us later to investigate that particular aspect of the problem.

It now remains to deal with the inner reality. Man has a wholly new type of mind. He is social and capable of speech. He generalizes, and he has a very highly developed power of association. This combination gives him a great many possibilities

hitherto denied to life.   In the first place, he is able
to order his experiences in a totally new way, differing from the old very much as a classified card-
index differs from a rough diary-record of events.
The organization of his mind is elastic, capable of indefinite expanion and of specialization in any direction

That being so, there will be always parts of his
mind wholly or at least partially undeveloped; and
in any case the capacities which he must employ in
his everyday life, the region of his mind illuminated
by the attention needed in the struggle for existence,
constitute but a fraction of his mental self and its
potentialities.

This brings us on to one of the most important
achievements of modern psychology—the discovery
and analysis of the subconscious.   Impossible here
to go into detail; we must content ourselves with
a few broad statements.   When we speak of the subconscious mind, we mean that in man there exist
processes which appear for many reasons to be of
the same nature as those of the normal mind (in that
they are associated with the same parts of the nervous system, fulfil the same general biological functions, and probably operate through similar mechanisms), with the single exception that we are not
conscious of them as such.[7]

The conscious mind, that which we think of as

[7] See Prince, '06 and '16; Freud, '22; Jung, '19; Rivers, '20;
Brown, '22.

the basis of our mental individuality, as our personal being, is the result of a long process of organization. We come into the world with a set of instinctive and emotional reactions only waiting their proper stimuli to be fired off, with a capacity for learning, for amassing experience, and a capacity for modifying our instincts and our behaviour according to our experience. We incorporate experience in ourselves, and in so doing we alter the original basis of our reactions, a strongly emotional experience colours all that is closely associated with it; and so after birth we are continually making our mental microcosm not only larger but qualitatively more complex, in exactly the same way as before birth our body grew not only in size, but also in complexity of organization.

Parts of experience or of inherited tendencies may fail to become organically connected with the main parts of our minds, simply because attention has never been focussed on them, or has not attempted to bring them into relation with the rest. They are, shall we say, like bricks which might have been used in a building, but have been left lying on the ground by the workmen.

Still more remarkable are the methods by which harmony is achieved in the personal mind. It is obvious that a conflict of any sort between parts of the mind will waste energy, will prevent a clear-cut reaction being given in either direction, and so constitute a grave biological disadvantage by making us fall between two stools. If a child gets a serious fright in the dark, darkness will tend to arouse fear. But darkness also comes with evening and with the time for sleep. Two modes of reaction to darkness are therefore given, and they are self-contradictory. One part of the mind comes down its pathway towards action, and finds itself met by another which is coming along the same path in the opposite direction. If neither moves, there is a conflict; in our hypothetical case sleep is delayed; and if it comes, is disturbed by nightmares—the echoes of the fright —and the childish organism suffers.

Exactly similar conflicts in which fear plays a part may occur in adult life, e.g., in so-called "shell-shock"; or the sex-instinct may come into conflict with other parts of the personality.

These conflicts are resolved through one tendency or part of experience being passed into the subconscious, where it no longer can meet its opponent on the path to action. And this passage into the subconscious can be apparently automatic, unwitting, when it is called *suppression,* or performed only by voluntary effort, when it is called *repression* In the former case, it would appear that the conflict may wholly or almost wholly cease, whereas in the second, the repressed portion of mind is perpetually striving to come to the surface again, and must thus perpetually be held down by force.

If we hold by our metaphor of the building, then in suppression, bricks which would not go well with the rest are stacked quietly in the cellars; while in repression, part of the workmen want to build a different sort of building, and have to be forcibly held down by some of the rest to prevent their doing so.

But in whatever way the subconscious may be organized it is always with us, and there will always be a remainder of our soul, or of its possibilities, which is not incorporated in our personal life at all, as well as much which is not closely organized with the main everyday personality, but is connected with it only by vague and loose bonds, approachable only by narrow pathways instead of by broad roads.

There is another process at work in the human mind which is of the utmost importance for our problem. I mean the process of sublimation. If it is not easy to give a short and clear definition of sublimation, at least the process is familiar to all. The commonest example is "falling in love," where the simple sex-instinct becomes intertwined with other instincts and with past emotional experience, and projects itself in wholly new guise upon its object. We may perhaps best say that a sublimated instinct has more and higher values attached to its satisfaction than one unsublimated. The mere satisfaction of the sexual impulse need be little more than a physiological desirability; but the satisfaction of passionate love involves every fibre of the mental organism, hopes and ideals converging with memories and instincts on to the highest pitch of being.

In such a case sublimation occurs with the normal object of the instinct. But the elasticity of man's mind permits of further complication; the instinct may be not only sublimated but attached to new objects. Through the cogs and spirals of the mind, the sexual instinct may find an outlet at higher levels, and contribute to the driving force of adventurous living, of art, or as we may see in many mystics—St. Teresa for example—of religious ecstasy.

It is as if a swift stream were falling into underground channels below the mill of our being, where it could churn and roar away to waste. But some of it is led off at a higher level, and we can learn to lead off still more; and we can make an installation of pipes whereby it can be taken up to the original level, and made to fall through new machines and do any work we may ask of it.

The mechanism of sublimation, however, deserves a few more words. Recent work in biology has shown that in low forms of animals and in early stages of high forms, the head-region is in a certain sense dominant to the rest, in that it forms first and independently; but that, once present, it exerts a formative influence upon the rest of the body, keeping the various organs in some way under control, making them different from what they would otherwise have been, and so moulding them to the part of a single and higher whole.

An extremely similar process is at work in sublimation. Ideas and ideals can be naturally dominant over others, or they can become dominant through becoming associated with primarily dominant ideas, or by receiving a larger share of attention. Attention, concentration, what you will, is one of the most remarkable mental functions. Not only can the metaphor of intense illumination of a particular field be justly used of it, but we may say that it seems to accelerate the flow of menal process through a particular channel, and so to draw into that channel the contents of other channels in connection with it, just as a rapid flow of water through a pipe sucks in water from connected pipes.

As a result of this, sublimation involves not the suppression or repression of instincts and emotional experiences, nor merely the summation of them with another instinct, but their utilization as parts of a new whole, of which the dominant instinct is like the controlling head.

When the sex-instinct is repressed, the emotional and religious life is meagre, though often violent. When the sex-instinct and the religious feeling exist side by side, without conflict but without union, you have "the natural man" of St. Paul; but when the religious ideals are dominant, and can catch up the sex-instinct into themselves, and in so doing give it a new form and a new direction, then you get one of the highest types of emotional lives. Or fear may be sublimated to reverence; or sex again to art or to philanthropy.

In every case, a new and more complicated mental

activity or organ is arrived at; and the same process that we saw at work in biological evolution—the creation of ever more complex units—is thereby continued.

Then we come to the fact that man displays disharmonies of mental construction, together with an innate hankering after harmony. The most obvious disharmony is that between the instincts that are self-regarding and those that are other-regarding—between man's egotistic and his social tendencies.

It appears that man became gregarious quite late in evolutionary history. Through natural selection, sufficient "herd-instinct" was developed to ensure that men would on the whole stand by the tribe in danger, that the tribe should become a real biological unit. But it was impossible wholly to harmonize these new social instincts, even in the simplest societies, with the old, deeper-rooted, individualist tendencies, and as life became more complex and choice wider, conflict grew more and more frequent.[8]

Another obvious disharmony in modern civilized communities is the fact that sexual maturity occurs long before marriage is possible or desirable.

In all this, there is inevitably a field for all the various combinations of suppression, or repression, or sublimation.

Man's gregariousness, together with his power of speech, learning, and generalization, have led to the development of a new thing in the world—persistent

[8] See Trotter, '19.

and cumulative tradition. I use tradition in the broadest sense, as denoting all that owes its being to the mind of man, and is handed down, by speech or imitation or in some permanent record, from generation to generation. Language, general ideas of right and wrong, convention, invention, national feeling—all this and much more, constituting the more important part of the human individual's environment —is part of tradition; and tradition is pre-eminently and inevitably social However individualistic we may wish to be we cannot escape modelling by this social environment.

The general effect of man's gregarious instinct is that he desires to find himself in harmony with some traditions, with the ideas that modern jargon likes to call the herd to which he belongs. The herd ideas, the traditions, may be those of a nation or of a stratum within the nation; of a whole class or of a clique; of science or of art; of a retired monasticism, or of an all-embracing world-civilization. But they are always herd ideas, and through them man is always member of some community, even though that community be tiny, or consist mainly of writers dead and gone; and he always strives to put himself in harmony with the traditions of that community.

* * * * * * *

A long-winded introduction enough; now for the bearing of it. One of the essentials of every religion is its treatment of the subconscious, is its view and its practice as regards the relation between the personally-organized part of the mind to the remaining non-personal reservoirs. At first the non-personal part is regarded as being wholly outside the organism, and its occasional flooding up into the narrower ego is regarded as an operation of an external personality, a spirit, a God. Comparatively late, it is recognized as part of the organism, but the process by which connection is made is still regarded as divine, and called inspiration. Such ideas belong to the adolescence of the race, in precisely the same way as the discovery and acquisition of great tracts of this subconscious territory will always necessarily constitute part of the adolescence of the individual. But any developed religion must always in some way help to make these great reserves of power accessible, always teach the enlargements of the personal ego which their conquest brings about. This is one of the ways in which, to use current religious phraseology, self may be lost, and found again on a different plane.

Religion must further always provide some internal harmony, in counterpart to the harmony demanded in the unitary comprehension of external reality. The various activities and experiences of life, as they are originally given by heredity to the child, are either independent, or else antagonistic and disharmonious. There must be some means provided for bringing all of them into a true organization—in other words into a whole which, though yet single, is composed of co-operating parts. Here again the actual responses of actual religions have been many and various; but they all operate by suppression, repression, and sublimation, or by a combination of these

It can at once be said that sublimation is the right and highest way, and that two of the criteria of religious progress are to be found in the stress laid upon sublimation, and in the enlargement and the elevation of the dominant ideas at work in the sublimating process. It is the right and highest way because through it no spiritual energy is wasted, and the age-long path of progress towards ever higher levels of complexity in organization is still continued Among religious teachers, both Jesus and Paul laid great stress on this—on the freedom, the emancipation from the shackles of an external law made possible by the apprehension of some highest harmonizing principle and the subordination of all other ideas and desires to it. Once one can see and learn to follow such a principle, whatever one does is in a sense right, because one's desires are all subordinate to a desire for right, and to something which is right. Perhaps it would be better to say that they appear right to oneself, that the haunting, terrible sense of sin is laid to rest, and one's life liberated into free activity, one's energy made all available for achievement.

The sense of sin, if not universal at one or other period of life, is almost so, and comes from an apprehension of inner disharmony. As one would expect, selfishness and sex are its most common roots; and whenever it exists, then the necessary preliminary to any further progress of one's being is that it should be made to disappear. It can disappear, as in St. Paul's natural man, by a suppression of part of the mind or of the connection between parts, or by a failure to make certain connections, or it can be eradicated by a growth of callousness; or—and I take it that this is the proper religious solution—by discovering a clue which will harmonize the two apparently opposed sections of experience, the two antagonistic tendencies, and so resolve the problem with no loss of energy or of vital possibilities.

*　　*　　*　　*　　*　　*　　*

Finally, there remains to be considered the mode in which the mind may best organize the ideas of external reality given to it by its pure cognitive and intellectual faculties.

Even from the purely scientific point of view, generalization is obviously of value. When we have found unity in the outer world's apparent diversity, direction in its apparent disorderliness, we have obviously achieved a great gain. But religion appears to demand something more. If for a moment we look at the matter pragmatically, we shall find that a number of the great mystics (and a large majority of those of our own occidental type and tradition) speak of their experiences of "divine communion" as being communion with a *person.*

What does this mean? We have seen that a purely intellectual analysis gives us no handle for finding personality in God. Can we suppose that this direct intuition gives us that handle? To say so, to my mind, would be simple obscurantism. Intuition, if it shows us reality, can only show a reality capable in the long run of intellectual analysis; to deny this is to deny all our premisses. No: their intuition shows us that something akin to personality is perceived, but permits no pronouncement as to whether its resemblance to personality is given in its real nature, or introduced into it by their thought.

If we look into the history of religion, we find over and over again that man has taken something from his own mind and projected it into the external world. The magic power of fetishes, the tabus incurred by contact with certain objects, the endowment of the idea of external powers, of God, with human form, the ascription of miraculous influence to places or things—in every case there has been this projection. And there is no reason to doubt that here again there has been a similar occurrence, that man has organized his idea of external power after the pattern of a personality, and has then ascribed this type of organization to the external power itself. This projection Blake symbolized in a sentence: "Thus men forgot that All Deities reside in the Human breast."

The rival schools of psychology may disagree: but all are agreed that some modes of thinking are more primitive than others, and even in the most educated amongst us tend to persist, often in the subconscious, side by side with more developed methods that have arisen later.

The use of concrete symbols or images is the most widespread of these primitive modes of thought. It is natural that the more complex should at the first be described in terms of the less complex, that those experiences for which no proper terminology has been hammered out should be given names out of man's existing vocabulary. That is inevitable: but there is an even more fundamental process at work. It seems as if the human mind works, on its most primitive levels, by means of image-formation, and that emotions and concepts for which no simple image exist may call up symbolic images by association and indeed often dress themselves in these new clothes before they present themselves to consciousness. Some such process appears to take place in dreams (including day-dreams!) and possibly in the ordinary thought-processes of savages. More advanced modes of thought substitute the currency of an arbitrary token such as a word or a formula for the barter of images and concrete symbols; the freshness and vividness of the image is lost, but more efficient and speedier working is attained. However, in most of us the concrete image-using mode of thought is a relief from the apparently less natural and more artificial (though more efficient) operations of reason, and we relapse into it, wholly or partially, more often than we realize.

This unconscious irrational tendency to symbolism, together with the other tendency to project ideas properly attaching to the subjective world into external objects and processes—these between them account for much of the modes of expression so far found for religious belief; and, since the majority of human beings have a profound distaste for sustained or difficult thought, it is likely that they will continue to account for much in the future.

These are facts of extreme importance. The professional sceptic is at once tempted to exclaim that every such projection and illogical symbolism is illusion through and through, and must be wholly swept aside. He would be wrong. We each of us must know from our own experience the "influence" (to use a general term) which may inhere in certain things and places. True that the influence is of our own mind's making; but it is none the less real, not only as a momentary existence, but, as the term implies, as exerting a definite and often a great effect upon our lives. The lover who cherishes a ring or a lock of hair; the man who is drawn back to the haunts of his childhood or his youth; the mind refreshing itself with some loved poem or picture;— what do we have in these and innumerable other instances but a peculiarity of mind whereby it may take external objects into itself and invest them with its own emotions and ideas, in such a way that those same objects may later reflect their stored-up emotion back again into the mind? It operates by a form of association; but the actual working resembles the charging of a battery, which may subsequently discharge back. We have in it, in fact, a special faculty which, if rightly used, is of the greatest practical value. Further, the symbol, if rightly used and rightly limited, is of service to most minds in giving a more or less concrete cage for the winged, elusive, and hardly-retained creatures of abstract thought.

So too, the organization of the idea of God into a form resembling a personality appears definitely to have, at least with the majority of people belonging to what we call "Western civilization," a real value.

Biologically, the essence of real personality is first that it is organized, and secondly that on each of its many faces it can, if I may put it metaphorically, enter into action at a single point, but with its whole content of energy available behind the point. In other words, man as a personality can concentrate his mind on one particular problem of one special aspect of reality, but he is able, if need be, to summon up ever fresh reinforcements if he cannot carry the position—more facts, other ways of thinking and feeling, memories, reserves of will. In a properly organized personality, it is possible to bring the whole to bear upon any single object.

Now when the idea which man makes for himself of outer reality is organized after the same general pattern as a personality, it too will be able to act in this same sort of way.

When man in perplexity interrogates the idea he has of external reality, he is anxious to put his little individual self in harmonious relation with the whole of reality that he knows. Therefore he should organize that reality as a whole, and in such a way that it can all be brought to bear through any single point. The relation between the self and the idea of outer reality is, for any one problem, that of two pyramids touching by their points only, but the points of contact can shift as by miracle over their surfaces as the problem is changed.

But another power of personalities is their power of interpenetration. The purely material cannot do this. One portion of matter cannot occupy the same space as a second portion. It is another of the great differences between the psychozoic and all previous stages of evolution, between man and all else that we know in the universe, that the discrete units reached at this level of organization, the individual human beings, can achieve interpenetration by means of their minds. When you expound a new idea to me, and I grasp it, our minds have obviously interpenetrated. This is a simple case; but there may be an intimate union of mind with mind which is the basis of the highest spiritual achievement and the greatest happiness. If mind and matter are two properties of the same world-substance, then the rise of mind to dominance has enabled this basic substance to escape from some of the imprisoning limitations which confined it at lower levels of its development; do we not all know that despair at being boxed up, that craving for communion? Using ou:

previous line of argument, we see that the interpenetration of personalities is right, implies a further
step in progress, must be part of the basis on which
future advance in evolution is to build.

But to apply this to our present point. By organizing our knowledge of outer reality after the pattern
of a personality, we make it possible for it to interpenetrate our private personality. If, therefore, we
have, in any true sense of the word, "found religion,"
it means that we shall so have organized our minds
that, for flashes at least, we attain to a sense of interpenetration with the reality around us—that reality
which includes not only the celestial bodies, or the
rocks and waters, not only evolving life, but also
other human beings, also ideas, also ideals.

This, to my mind, is what actually happens when
men speak of communion with God. It is a setting,
an organizing of our experiences of the universe in
relation with the driving forces of our soul or mental
being, so that the two are united and harmonized.
There is a resolution of conflicts, an attainment of a
profound serenity, a conviction that the experience
is of the utmost value and importance.

Up till now, we have been defining and analysing:
here we see religion in operation. It is a relation
of the personality as a unit to external reality as a
unit—and a relation of harmony. First, the inner
structure of the mind must be organized into a harmonious unit, then our knowledge of outer reality
organized similarly, and finally, in religious experi-

ence, the two must be harmonized in interpenetrating union.

Once this harmony has been achieved, it is for one thing so precious in itself that it will be sought for again; the knowledge that we have once reached the stage at which difficulties and doubts are resolved in what the philosophers would perhaps call a higher unity, but which I should prefer to call an organic harmony, is always there to fall back upon in times of discouragement; and finally the harmony is actually woven into the tissue of our mind, just as the amazing physical harmony revealed by physiology has, in the course of evolution, been woven into the structure and working of living bodies; and it can remain there as the dominant idea to which the rest of our ideas, and consequently our actions, are brought into subordinate relation. In other words, it becomes the dominant sublimating principle. Once more, however, the subordination is not forced, but free—we find that what we once thought obstacles are aids, what once seemed sin is now the willing and efficient handmaid of good. That is the fundamental fact in all genuine and valuable religious experience as such—the resolution of conflict and the losing, or enlarging as you will, of the private personality, the mere "self." You will find this set out more fully, though in different terminology, in Miss Underhill's books on mysticism, or in William James's *Varieties of Religious Experience,* or in Thouless's *Psychology of Religion.*

One side-issue. Such experience, if not absolute in the philosophical sense, is absolute for us. If I may be Irish, its absoluteness is relative to our organization and to reality as we perceive it. We cannot perceive anything fuller, more absolute—until perhaps one day, with the growth of our minds, we come to have some still richer and more complete experience. As William James was so fond of reminding the world, we have no right to assume that our minds are, much less that they must be, the highest type of mind realized in the universe—no more right than our domestic animals have, although our minds to them could only be measured by their own standards.

What is more, owing to our power of framing general concepts and ideals, and of accumulating past and future in our present, we can focus a vast deal to one point. In such experiences, whether they come through religion, or love, or art, we may say that although we are but a system of relations, we touch the Absolute—although we are mortal, we mount to the Eternal for a moment. Only, to guard against error, we must remember that it is obviously not in reality the Absolute or the Eternal that we attain to, but only the nearest approximation to them of which we are capable.

We can therefore sum up this second part of our investigation by saying that religion, to be more than mere ritual, must involve the possibility of harmonizing the parts of the soul, of wiping out the sense of sin, of sublimating instinct, of rendering the subconscious reservoirs of energy and being available for the personal self, and of organizing the ideas of external reality into a single organized mental whole—the idea of God—capable of reacting with the personal self by interpenetration.

Although he was moving to quite other conclusions, it is worth recalling James's ideas. For instance, "The line of least resistance . . . is to accept the notion . . . that there is a God, but that he is finite. . . . These, I need hardly tell you, are the terms in which common men have usually carried on their active commerce with God, and the Monistic" [sc. Absolutist] "perfections that make the notion of him so paradoxical practically and morally are the colder addition of remote professorial minds operating *in distans* upon conceptual substitutes for him alone" (James, '09, p. 311.)

I may perhaps be rebuked for trying to analyse the unanalysable, for neglecting the supreme and sufficing fact of experience of God in favour of the unprofitable and impossible task of catching the infinite in an intellectual net. There are two answers to this. One is that unanalysed experience is selfish because less communicable: with that we deal later. The other is even more important: it is this. Humanity at large is *not* content with emotional experience alone, however complete and apparently satisfying it has always demanded an intellectual formulation of the reality with which it is in contact, as well as emotional experience of it, and so far as we can judge it will always continue to do so.

But it is further found, as matter again of general experience, that such formulations do not remain innocuous in the vacuum of pure intellect, but reverberate upon action and influence conduct. When men believe that they are surrounded with magical powers, they spend half their lives in ritual designed to affect the operations of these (wholly hypothetical) influences. When they worship a God whom they rationalize as man-like, they sacrifice a large proportion of their produce on his altars, and may even kill their fellow-creatures to placate his (again imaginary) passions. When they believe in a Divine Revelation, they think that they possess complete enlightenment on the great problems of life and death; and they will then cheerfully burn those who differ from them, or embark upon the bloodiest wars in defence of this imaginary certainty. When they worship God as absolute and as a person, they cannot help making deductions that lead them into absurdities of thought and of conduct: they deny or oppose ideas derived from a study of nature, the only actual source of knowledge, because they conflict with what they believe to be immutable truths, but are in reality conclusions drawn from false premisses; they tend to an acquiescent and obscurantist spirit in the belief that such moral and intellectual laziness is "doing God's will," when that will is in reality their own personification of cosmic direction.

Sooner or later, false thinking brings wrong conduct. Man can perhaps get along with empirical methods and ideas which turn out on analysis to be only symbols, provided that he does not attempt difficult construction. He can have some sort of a religion, which will be some sort of a help to him, even when its so-called certitudes are only a collection of mixed metaphors, in the same way as he can practise agriculture on a basis of mingled empiricism and superstition. But just as he is finding that he is only able to raise agricultural efficiency to its highest pitch by relying on the result of scientific method, as when he uses synthetic nitrates instead of ploughing in a leguminous crop, or just as a power-station would be very difficult to run if the staff had only symbolic ideas on the nature of electricity no closer to the real than is the symbolism of most religions, so if he does not bring scientific analysis into the intellectual side of his religion, he cannot realize religious possibilities. True that in a sense all knowledge and intellectual presentation is symbolic: but there is the world of difference between the merely analogical symbolism which takes one idea or thing as symbolic of another because there is some degree of similarity between the two and the first is more familiar, and the scientific symbolism which strives to find a scientific counter, so to speak, which shall represent particular phenomena as closely as possible, and them alone.

Not only this, but religion unillumined by reason

degenerates into an evil thing. Religion seems to be
a natural activity and need of the average human
mind. But when its more primitive components are
allowed to dominate, when the instinctive and emotional in it are unchecked by reflection and rational
thought, then, as history too clearly shows us, it becomes a cruel and obstructive power. To the fine
mind of Lucretius, the religion that he knew was
the greatest enemy:—

> "Quae caput a caeli regionibus ostendebat
> Horribili super aspecta mortalibus instans"

And he replies to the charge of impiety by pointing
to the foul deeds perpetrated by religion:

> "—Quod contra saepius illa
> Religio peparit scelerosa atque impia facta."

Many another thinker and reformer has felt the same.

There are those who, like Jung, believe that religion is an illusion but also a necessity to the bulk
of mankind, and therefore should be encouraged.
But the broader and truer view, I believe, is the one
we have adopted. We have seen that, in man, evolution has reached a new plane, on which not only
have new aims and values appeared, but the possibility of new and better evolutionary methods has
arisen. These new methods are only possible, however, in so far as life, in man, uses her new gifts
The progress of civilization is a constant conflict
between that part of man which he shares with the
beasts and that part which is his alone—between
man as no more than a new kind of animal and man

as a rational and spiritual being.   In so far as religion is irrational, it is no more than a dog baying the moon, no higher activity than the nocturnal concerts of Howler monkeys, no more and no less moral than the nobility of birds or beasts to a strangely-marked or unusually-built member of their species, or the sense of being a trespasser so often shown by a bird that has ventured upon the nesting-territory of another.   Recall the "Natural Religion" of Robert Browning's *Caliban;* on which plane did that grow? But when we have discovered its real bases, and subordinated its impulsive promptings to the control of reason and of the new, higher values in which reason must always share—then it becomes an instrument for helping in the conquest of the new regions which lie open to man as individual and as species.   And in this it resembles every other human activity without exception.

In religion the danger has always been that analogy and symbolism be taken for more than they are—for scientific knowledge, or even for an absolute certainty of some still higher order—and conclusions then drawn from it.   The conclusions follow with full syllogistic majesty: but their feet are of clay—their premisses are false.

If we find that this is the case to-day, we not only may but we must endeavour to make our formulation correspond more closely with reality, must not be content to take one thing in place of another, the familiar for the unfamiliar, must set about destroying the old false formulation for fear of the further harm that it will do by its hold upon man's incurable habit of drawing conclusions.

Nor does this in any way interfere with or detract from the private and unique experiences that in the long run *are* religion. They remain; but they are thus hindered from becoming draped with delusion, from leading their possessor into false courses.

We may put it in another way. Too often in the past, religious experience has been one-sided—one-or-other-sided instead of two-sided. The intellectually-inclined, the theologians, frame more or less adequate ideas of external reality, but fail in the majority of cases to set their own house in order, to organize the inner reality to react with the outer; they have theory without practice, are Dry-as-dusts. On the other hand, the emotionally-minded who are gifted besides with organizing and intuitive power, the mystics—they build up their own souls into a desired and lovely edifice, in which too they have constructed a spiritual machinery capable of viewing external realities on a new plane, under a more highly synthesized aspect; but they neglect the precise analysis of that outer reality, and so can only speak in the barest symbols and metaphors, and cannot put their hard-won knowledge into a form available for others. They have that non-communicable skill which is that of the craftsman alone as opposed to the craftsman who is also in some degree a scientist We know good mysticism from bad, as we know good art from bad—as definitely and as personally. And we are sure that good mysticism, like good art, is somehow of supreme, transcendent importance; but almost always it has remained like a purely symbolic art, not having for others the value which it should have or did have for the mystic himself, because not properly enchained, as the French say, with stern and immutable fact. And of the theologian we feel that he gives us the grammar, not the spirit, that he does not help us toward the supremely important act of experiencing, but only to understanding experience if we chance to have had it.

One word on the problem of transcendence. The mystic will tell us that transcendence is a hall-mark of religion at its highest. His mode of experience transcends normal experience; things of everyday life become surcharged with new, transcendent values; he has transcended from a plane of disharmony to one of harmony. But the mystic is not alone in this. Familiar examples are best examples: and the transcendence of the lover's experience is so familiar that all mankind is divided into those who have it, those who long for it, and those who laugh at it. But the great philosopher too must mediate between the transcendent and mankind, and the true artist also, and the moralist worthy of the name.

What goes under this technical name of transcendence, therefore, is the product of some special psychological mechanism which may be at work in the most diverse spheres. It we wish to substitute one technical phrase for another, we can say that it consists in the successful attachment of what we have called absolute value to some human activity, so as to make it for the time at least unitary, dominant, and all-embracing. But psychologically speaking the genesis of "absolute values" depends upon the generalizing of particular values; the raising of them to the highest possible pitch, and the putting of them and the rest of the mental organization into a relation in which they are permanently or temporarily the dominating head and front, and are connected with and gain strength and support from all the rest of the mind.

The problem of transcendence, in other words, is not one of divine inspiration, of wholly mysterious experience, but one special case of the problem of sublimation; and as such it is to be investigated by psychological science, to be understood, to be democratized, to be made more available to all who wish for it.

The most ardent enemies of traditional religion have often professed the most transcendental type of morality. Some men are pragmatic and utilitarian in regard to Truth; by others she is worshipped as fanatically as any goddess. So some men deliberately make *mariages de convenance;* to others, the transcendence of their love is such that they precipitate themselves into what can only be described as *mariages d'inconvenance.*

I have dilated upon this at some length, because

those whom we may call the religious writers on religion so often lay such stress on this question of transcendence and its special value and importance. But you do not—in the long run at least—make a thing more important by giving it an imposing title; you only give it a false exclusiveness.

Transcendence is the experimental side of what we have been describing all along: it is the finding of unity in diversity, the synthesis of discord in harmony and in especial the finding of something of supreme value (and therefore dominant) which can be linked up with the whole extent of our mental being. Transcendence in religion differs from transcendence in art or love only in its objects. In love the discrepancy between the object and the ideal values hung round it is often so glaring as to provoke laughter from cynics, compassion from the rest. In art, the operations by which an artist turns a collection of mean and commonplace objects into a beautiful and single whole, a poet invests failure and death with authentic tragedy, or drags every-day to a seat in eternity, are just as transcendent as that by which the mystic converts the relation between the warring passions of his soul and the infinite catalogue of differences which he finds around him into what he can only speak of as a divine communion, all-satisfying in itself, all-important for the conduct of his life. Science can here help religion by analysing and interpreting phenomena such as transcendence, paring the false from the true, cutting down false claims, substituting the hopefulness of natural causation for the illogical vagaries of supernaturalism and incommunicability.

*   *   *   *   *   *   *

I may perhaps be allowed to close with a few more practical aspects of the problem.

Many religious ideas and practices, as man's thought clarified itself, have proved to be unserviceable, and have been thrown on the lumber-heap, or left only with the losers in the race. It is impossible for any educated man nowadays to believe in the efficacy of magic, or of animal sacrifice; to accept the first chapter of Genesis as literally true; or to believe that God has human parts and passions. But there was a time when all these could be, and were, believed.

The time is obviously coming when a great many other ideas must be cast aside in favour of new ones. If you have followed me, you will agree that it is impossible for me and those who think like me to believe in God as a person, a ruler, to continue to speak of God as a spiritual *Being* in the ordinary way. Consequently, although the value of prayer persists in so far as it is meditative and a self-purification of the mind, yet its commonly accepted petitive value must fall to the ground; [9] so must all idea of miracle and of direct inspiration; so must all that is involved in the ordinary materialist ideas of ritual, self-denial, and worship as merely propitiation or

[9] See Turner, '16.

"acceptable incense"; so must all the externally-projected parts of the ideas concerning the ordaining of special priests; so must all notion of our having a complete, peculiar, or absolute knowledge of God, or of there being a divinely-appointed rule of conduct or a divinely-revealed belief.

On such matters, most advanced thinkers have been long in general agreement. But there is one very important point which, so far as I know, has been very little touched upon—chiefly, I think, because such radical thinkers have been for the most part destructive, and so have not envisaged this particular side of the question.

I hope I have been able to convince you that the scientific manner of thinking can lay the foundation for something constructive in religion: this great problem, however, remains: what sort of form or organization shall any such new-moulded religion take on itself?

We have just decided that fixed and rigid dogma is impossible, and that completeness is out of the question. Yet humanity craves for certainty and is not content to leave any factor out of the scheme of things.

To this we answer that it is here that real faith enters. We cannot know the absolute, nor have we discovered a goal for our efforts. But we have discovered a unity embracing all that we know, and a direction starting at the first moment to which our reconstructive thought can penetrate, continuing till to-day, and showing an acceleration of speed on which we may raise our hopes for the future.

We do not know all. For instance, I have studiously avoided ever mentioning the word *immortality*, since I believe that Science cannot yet profitably discuss that question. But the discovery of unity in all that has so far been studied gives us reasonable faith that its wings will reach out to cover all that we shall still be enabled to learn, while the unbroken continuity of evolutionary direction gives us the same sort of right to believe that it will continue to-morrow and on into time as we have to believe that apples will continue to fall to the earth.

The study of evolution may give us a further help. We have seen how the final steps of the highest forms of animals have been in the direction of plasticity of organization: we see it in the rise of man from mammals, in higher as against more primitive levels of human culture, in great men as against ordinary men. There can be no doubt that its acquisition constitutes a step in evolutionary progress. Plasticity is needed in any new religion. And plasticity means tolerance, means the reduction of fixity of ritual, of convention, of dogma, of clericalism.

It is clear that, as complexity increases, need will be felt for a finer adjustment of satisfaction to mood, a more delicate adaptation of religion to the individual. A few types of ceremony satisfied primitive races: an elaborate system, fixed in essence, fluctuating in detail, has grown up in modern Christianity.

But the more complex the mind, the less does it like to have to "wait till Sunday"—the less is it satisfied with the solely biblical point of view, or the literary and musical level of Hymns A. and M.

The less also is it satisfied with the mediation of a priest. Priest (or Priest-King) is sole mediator in most savage tribes: his mediation is enormously important in the Roman Catholic Church: less so in Protestant Churches: until with the progressive raising of the spiritual and cultural level, it is perhaps possible that he may become an obstacle instead of a help. Mediators there must always be. They are the great ones—prophets and poets, heroes, philosophers, musicians, artists, and all who discover or interpret or display what for the ordinary man is hidden or difficult or rare. They mediate between the utmost attainable by man and man in the lump. As Hegel says of one group of these mediators, the artists, it is the function of their art to deliver to the domain of feeling and delight of vision all that the mind may possess of essential and transcendent Being. But, with the spread of invention and the change of civilization, their mediations are becoming more and more readily accessible to all. I can get, on the whole, more satisfactory mediation from three or four feet of properly filled bookshelf than from a dozen priests. Milton will give me doctrine if I want it, but stupendously: Wordsworth will reveal nature: Shakespeare the hearts of men: Blake can put men into a mystical, Shelley into an intellectual ecstasy, while Keats and a dozen others can open universal doors of beauty. What is more, if I have had the mediation of wise parents and good teachers, or to be so fortunate as to be enthusiastic, I find that in many things I can be my own mediator, in the same way as the Protestant found that he could read his Bible and eat the holy bread and wine for himself as well or better than the priest could do it for him.

Whatever we may say or like, it is an obvious fact that much of what is essential in religious experience, which in a simpler society was only attainable in prayer and sacrifice, communal ceremony or ritual worship, is now attainable to an increasing degree through literature, music, drama, art, and is, again, as a matter of fact, so attained by an increasing number of people who do not profess a creed or belong to a church. So that, as regards the personal, individual side of religion, many of the functions of Churches will inevitably be better performed through direct contact between the individual and the mediator—philosopher, poet, artist, or whatever he be—who provides the experience

There remains public worship and community-religion. It is clear that whereas a Church in the Middle Ages was not only Church but also Museum of curiosities, Art-gallery and Theatre, and in large measure also took the place of our press and public libraries, now it is none of these things. There is now less reason for public worship, fewer functions for it to perform. On the other hand a religion is essentially in one aspect social, and not only does the unity of nature demand a unity of religion, but such unity of religion would be of the highest importance as a bond of civilization and a guarantee of the federalist as against the solely nationalist ideal. Moreover, to many types of mind, and to almost all men in certain circumstances, the partaking in a public religious ceremony in common with others is of real importance. It is safe to say, therefore, that these ceremonies will continue, however much modified, and that for them a mediator or priest, even if but temporarily acting as such, will be needed. The problem is largely that of combining in public worship the religious effectiveness of the simple, the hallowed, and the universally familiar—such as inheres in many of the prayers, psalms, and hymns of the Church to-day—with the spontaneity and immediacy which, for instance, are to be found at a devotional meeting of the Society of Friends.

In any case, the new intellectual premises once granted, the limitations imposed on human mind once understood, the important thing is to give a greater vigour and reality to religious experience itself, whether personal and private or social and public. It is just here that Science may help, where knowledge may be power. Atonement, conversion, sense of grace, ecstasy, prayer, sacrifice—the meaning and value of these and of other religious acts and experiences can be put on a proper psychological basis, they can be shorn of excrescences, and their practice take its place in normal spiritual development. That is of the essence of any religion rooted in scientific ideas—that comprehension should make practice easier and better worth while.

I am only too painfully aware of the omissions which such a cursory treatment of the subject inevitably involves. I have given you, I know, little but dry bones; but bones are the framework necessary before impatient life can animate a new form. If Science can construct that form, the emotions and hopes and energies of humanity will vivify and clothe it. It is with the aid of such intellectual scaffolding that the common mind of humanity in the future, inevitably rooted in scientific conceptions as it will be, must try to raise that much-desired building, a religion common to all.

In any case, I shall be more than content if I have been able to persuade you first that the term God, just as much as the terms Energy, say, or Justice, has a real meaning and scientifically-based sense. Second, that the idea of God has and will continue to have an important biological function in man as denoting an idea, organized in a particular way, of the whole of the reality with which he is in contact. Thirdly, that the physical and biological sciences, in discovering the unity of matter and energy, and the direction operating in cosmic evolution, have provided a real basis for what up till now have been only theological speculations. Fourthly, that psycholog-

ical science, in revealing some of the mechanism of
mind, is helping us to appreciate the value of so-
called mystical experience, is laying a foundation for
the proper spiritual training and development of human mind, and shows us how the idea of God may
be efficacious as a dominant idea in the all-important
process of sublimation. And finally that, since the
scientific mode of thought is of general and not
merely local or temporary validity, to build a religion on its basis is to make it possible for that religion to acquire a stability, a universality, and a
practical value hitherto unattained.

We are yet at the very beginning of that task, but
I cannot close better than by reminding you of another biological fact of importance, that from all
analogy the human species is yet near the beginning
of its evolutionary career, and that man has before
him vast tracts of time to set against the vastness of
his tasks.

A chapter in the history of Earth closed with the
appearance of Man. In man, the *Weltstoff* had been
made able to think and feel, to love beauty and
truth—the cosmos had generated soul. A new chapter then began, a chapter in which we all are characters. Matter had flowered in soul. Soul has
now to mould matter.

That moulding of matter by spirit is, under one
aspect, Science; under another, Art; under still another, Religion. Let us be careful not to allow
the moulding forces to counteract each other when
they might be made to co-operate.

BIBLIOGRAPHY

Arnold, M., '73, '75. "Literature and Dogma"; and "God and the Bible." London, 1873 and 1875

Baudouin, C , '20. "Suggestion and Auto-Suggestion" London, 1920.

Bergson, H , '11. "Creative Evolution." London, 1911.

Boutroux, E., '12 "Science and Religion in Contemporary Philosophy." London, 1912.

Brown, W., '22. "Psychology and Psychotherapy." London, 1922.

Buckland, '37. "Geology and Mineralogy considered with reference to Natural Theology." London, 1837.

Crawley, '02 "The Mystic Rose" London, 1902.

Danysz, J., '21. "La Genèse de l'Energie Psychique." Paris, 1921

Flaubert, G. "La Tentation de St Antoine."

Frazer, J. "The Golden Bough." 3 vols.

Freud, S , '13 "The Interpretation of Dreams" London, 1913. '14. "Psychopathology of Everyday Life." London, 1914.

Haldane, J S , '21. "Mechanism, Life, and Personality." London, 1921

Harrison, Jane, '09. "The Influence of Darwin on the Study of Religions" In Seward, '09, q v.

Huxley, T H "Evolution and Ethics Collected Essays." Vol. 9. London, 1906

James, W., '02. "Varieties of Religious Experience" London, 1902

——— '09 "A Pluralistic Universe." London, 1909

Jevons, '10. "The Idea of God in Early Religions." Cambridge, 1910.

Johnstone, J., '21. "The Mechanism of Life." London, 1921.

Jung, C. G., '18 and '20. "Psychology of the Unconscious" London, 1918; "Analytical Psychology." London, 1920.

Lloyd-Morgan, '23. "Emergent Evolution." London, 1923.

Lull, R. S., '17. "Organic Evolution." New York, 1917.

M'Dougall, W., '16. "Social Psychology" (10th Ed.). London, 1916.

Nicoll, '20. *In* "Functional Nerve Disease" (Ed. H. Crichton Miller). Oxford, 1920.

Prince, M., '06. "The Dissociation of a Personality." New York, 1906

—— —— '16. "The Unconscious." New York, 1916

Reinach, S., '09. "Orpheus; a General History of Religions." London, 1909.

Rivers, W. H., '20. "Instinct and the Unconscious." Cambridge, 1920.

Russell, Bertrand, '17. "A Free Man's Worship," *in* "Principles of Social Reconstruction" London, 1917.

Seward, A. C. (ed.), '09. "Darwin and Modern Science." Cambridge, 1909.

Thouless, '23. "Introduction to the Psychology of Religion." Cambridge, 1923.

Trotter, W., '19. "Instincts of the Herd in Peace and War" (2nd Ed.). London, 1919

Turner, A. C., '16. *In* "Concerning Prayer." By the author of "Pro Christo et Ecclesia" and Others. London, 1916.

Underhill, E., '20. "Essentials of Mysticism." London, 1920.

Webb, C. C. J., '18 "God and Personality." London, 1918.

Wells, H G , '17 "God the Invisible King." London, 1917.